KU-517-323

Adobe® Edge Animate

CLASSROOM IN A BOOK®

he official training workbo

KA 0384193 6

D-ROM Included for Windows and Ma

WITHDRAWN FROM
THE LIBRARY
UNIVERSITY OF
WINCHESTER

Adobe® Edge Animate Classroom in a Book®

© 2013 Adobe Systems Incorporated and its licensors. All rights reserved.

If this guide is distributed with software that includes an end user license agreement, this guide, as well as the software described in it, is furnished under license and may be used or copied only in accordance with the terms of such license. Except as permitted by any such license, no part of this guide may be reproduced, stored in a retrieval system, or transmitted, in any form or by any means, electronic, mechanical, recording, or otherwise, without the prior written permission of Adobe Systems Incorporated. Please note that the content in this guide is protected under copyright law even if it is not distributed with software that includes an end user license agreement.

The content of this guide is furnished for informational use only, is subject to change without notice, and should not be construed as a commitment by Adobe Systems Incorporated. Adobe Systems Incorporated assumes no responsibility or liability for any errors or inaccuracies that may appear in the informational content contained in this guide.

Please remember that existing artwork or images that you may want to include in your project may be protected under copyright law. The unauthorized incorporation of such material into your new work could be a violation of the rights of the copyright owner. Please be sure to obtain any permission required from the copyright owner.

Any references to company names in sample files are for demonstration purposes only and are not intended to refer to any actual organization.

Adobe, the Adobe logo, and Classroom in a Book are either registered trademarks or trademarks of Adobe Systems Incorporated in the United States and/or other countries.

Apple, Mac OS, Macintosh, and Safari are trademarks of Apple, registered in the U.S. and other countries. Microsoft, Windows, and Internet Explorer are either registered trademarks or trademarks of Microsoft Corporation in the U.S. and/or other countries. All other trademarks are the property of their respective owners.

Adobe Systems Incorporated, 345 Park Avenue, San Jose, California 95110-2704, USA

Notice to U.S. Government End Users. The Software and Documentation are "Commercial Items," as that term is defined at 48 C.F.R. §2.101, consisting of "Commercial Computer Software" and "Commercial Computer Software Documentation," as such terms are used in 48 C.F.R. §12.212 or 48 C.F.R. §227.7202, as applicable. Consistent with 48 C.F.R. §12.212 or 48 C.F.R. §§227.7202-1 through 227.7202-4, as applicable, the Commercial Computer Software and Commercial Computer Software Documentation are being licensed to U.S. Government end users (a) only as Commercial Items and (b) with only those rights as are granted to all other end users pursuant to the terms and conditions herein. Unpublished-rights reserved under the copyright laws of the United States. Adobe Systems Incorporated, 345 Park Avenue, San Jose, CA 95110-2704, USA. For U.S. Government End Users, Adobe agrees to comply with all applicable equal opportunity laws including, if appropriate, the provisions of Executive Order 11246, as amended, Section 402 of the Vietnam Era Veterans Readjustment Assistance Act of 1974 (38 USC 4212), and Section 503 of the Rehabilitation Act of 1973, as amended, and the regulations at 41 CFR Parts 60-1 through 60-60, 60-250, and 60-741. The affirmative action clause and regulations contained in the preceding sentence shall be incorporated by reference.

Adobe Press books are published by Peachpit, a division of Pearson Education located in San Francisco, California. For the latest on Adobe Press books, go to www.adobepress.com. To report errors, please send a note to errata@peachpit.com. For information on getting permission for reprints and excerpts, contact permissions@peachpit.com.

Acquisitions Editor: Rebecca Gulick
Writer: Russell Chun
Development and Copy Editor: Stephen Nathans-Kelly
Production Coordinator: Myrna Vladic
Compositor: David Van Ness
Technical Reviewer: Joseph Labrecque
Keystroker: H. Paul Robertson
Proofreader: Patricia Pane
Indexer: Rebecca Plunkett
Cover Designer: Eddie Yuen
Interior Designer: Mimi Heft

Printed and bound in the United States of America

ISBN-13:   978-0-321-84260-2
ISBN-10:   0-321-84260-X

9 8 7 6 5 4 3 2 1

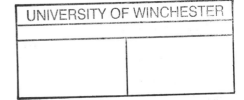

UNIVERSITY OF WINCHESTER

WHAT'S ON THE DISC

Here is an overview of the contents of the Classroom in a Book disc

The *Adobe Edge Animate Classroom in a Book* disc includes the lesson files that you'll need to complete the exercises in this book, as well as other content to help you learn more about Adobe Edge Animate and use it with greater efficiency and ease. The diagram below represents the contents of the disc, which should help you locate the files you need.

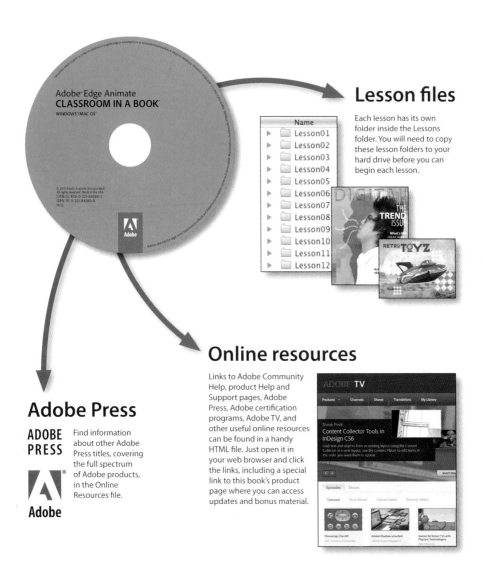

Lesson files

Each lesson has its own folder inside the Lessons folder. You will need to copy these lesson folders to your hard drive before you can begin each lesson.

Online resources

Links to Adobe Community Help, product Help and Support pages, Adobe Press, Adobe certification programs, Adobe TV, and other useful online resources can be found in a handy HTML file. Just open it in your web browser and click the links, including a special link to this book's product page where you can access updates and bonus material.

Adobe Press

Find information about other Adobe Press titles, covering the full spectrum of Adobe products, in the Online Resources file.

CONTENTS

UNIVERSITY OF WINCHESTER
LIBRARY

INTRODUCTION

Adobe Edge Animate is a new tool that provides a comprehensive authoring environment for creating animated, interactive, and media-rich content for the Web. Based on open, modern browser standards using HTML5, CSS3, and JavaScript, your Edge Animate creations run seamlessly across desktops, smartphones, and tablets. There is no need for the Flash Player, Silverlight, QuickTime, or downloading of any apps.

Use Edge Animate to build animated banner ads, dynamic websites, and even interactive games with the full capabilities of JavaScript.

Veteran Flash Professional users and animators will feel at home with a familiar interface consisting of a Timeline, Stage, and Library panel. They'll add motion to images and HTML elements such as text and simple shapes with property-based keyframing, easing, and nested animations. Coders at all levels of experience can add interactivity with the built-in code snippets or with JavaScript. With sophisticated, yet intuitive controls for development, and platform-independent content, Adobe Edge Animate will be sure to expand your creative reach.

Why Adobe Edge Animate?

Adobe Edge Animate represents the next step in the evolution of interactive and animated Web content development. With the growing adoption of HTML5 standards, modern browsers are now able to display rich media without the need for plug-ins, such as the Flash Player. In conjunction with CSS3 and JavaScript, Edge Animate enables users to integrate animation and complex interactivity for stunning visuals and engaging user experiences.

Unfortunately, the rapid rise in the popularity of HTML5, CSS3, and JavaScript has not coincided with the emergence of tools specifically for creative professionals. Coding motion graphics and interactive content by hand has been the usual course, but that approach takes time and effort, and for designers and animators who are more accustomed to graphical user interfaces, it's more difficult. Adobe Edge Animate opens the door to designers and animators by providing an intuitive interface and a familiar toolbox: tools for creating shapes, options for styling, transformations, precision layout, and typography, and a timeline with keyframe controls for motion graphics. Rather than spend time on coding, designers and animators can spend their energies on what they do best: designing and animating.

The Adobe family

How does Adobe Edge Animate differ from other Adobe tools for the Web? Although there are overlaps in capabilities, each application has its own strengths and support different technologies. Edge Animate shines particularly when it comes to creating motion graphics and interactive sites with HTML5, CSS3, and JavaScript. Adobe Dreamweaver, another application that creates Web content with HTML5 and CSS3, is intended more for overall site design and navigation. For example, you would create an animated banner ad in Edge Animate, and use Dreamweaver to integrate the banner ad within the larger site.

Adobe Flash Professional and Flash Builder are two other tools for creating animated and interactive content. However, both rely on the ActionScript programming language rather than HTML, CSS3, and JavaScript for interactivity. They both require the Flash Player or Adobe AIR to play Flash content. The Flash Player, although pervasive (it comes pre-installed with Google's Chrome browser), is not supported in all devices, and is not an open standard. However, the benefits of using the Flash Player or AIR are a uniform experience across all browsers, and the delivery of robust control—for example, with controlling your webcam or saving files to your desktop.

About Classroom in a Book

Adobe Edge Animate Classroom in a Book is part of the official training series for Adobe graphics and publishing software developed with the support of Adobe product experts. The lessons are designed so you can learn at your own pace. You'll learn the fundamental concepts and features you'll need to use the program.

Classroom in a Book also teaches many advanced features, including tips and techniques that will help you get the most out of Adobe Edge Animate.

Prerequisites

Before you begin using *Adobe Edge Animate Classroom in a Book*, make sure your system is set up correctly and that you've installed the required software. You should have a working knowledge of your computer and operating system. You should know how to use the mouse and standard menus and commands, and also how to open, save, and close files. If you need to review these techniques, see the printed or online documentation included with your Microsoft Windows or Apple Mac OS software.

Installing Edge Animate

You must purchase the Adobe Edge Animate software as a download from Adobe Creative Cloud. The following specifications are the minimum required system configurations:

Windows

- Intel® Pentium® 4 or AMD Athlon® 64 processor
- Windows 7 or Windows Vista® (Windows XP is NOT supported)
- 1 GB of RAM
- 200 MB of available hard-disk space for installation
- 1280x800 display with 16-bit video card
- Broadband Internet connection for online services and to validate Subscription Edition (if applicable) on an ongoing basis.

Mac OS

- Multicore Intel processor
- Mac OS X v10.6 and v10.7 (Mac OS X 10.5 is NOT supported)
- 1 GB of RAM
- 200 MB of available hard-disk space for installation
- 1280x800 display with 16-bit video card
- Broadband Internet connection for online services and to validate Subscription Edition (if applicable) on an ongoing basis.

For updates on system requirements and complete instructions on installing the software, visit http://adobe.com/edge.

Copying the lesson files

The lessons in *Adobe Edge Animate Classroom in a Book* use specific source files, such as image files created in Adobe Photoshop and prepared Edge Animate documents. To complete the lessons in this book, you must copy these files from the

Adobe Edge Animate Classroom in a Book CD-ROM to your hard drive. Follow these steps to copy the lesson files:

1 On your hard drive, create a new folder in a convenient location and name it **Edge_Animate_CIB**, following the standard procedure for your operating system:

   • **Windows:** In Explorer, select the folder or drive in which you want to create the new folder and choose File > New > Folder. Then type the new name.

   • **Mac OS:** In the Finder, choose File > New Folder. Type the new name and drag the folder to the location you want to use.

2 Drag the Lessons folder (which contains folders named Lesson01, Lesson02, and so on) from the *Adobe Edge Animate Classroom in a Book* disc onto your hard drive to your new Edge_Animate_CIB folder.

When you begin each lesson, navigate to the folder with that lesson number to access all the graphics, images, and other project files you need to complete the lesson.

If you have limited storage space on your computer, you can copy each lesson folder as you need it, and then delete it after you've completed the lesson if desired. Some lessons build on preceding lessons. In those cases, a starting project file is provided for you for the second lesson or project. You do not have to save any finished project if you don't want to or if you have limited hard-drive space.

Copying the sample projects

You will create and publish HTML files and related JavaScript files in the lessons in this book. The files in the End folders (01End, 02End, and so on) within the lesson folders are samples of completed projects for each lesson. Use these files for reference if you want to compare your work in progress with the project files used to generate the sample movies. The end project files vary in size, so you can either copy them all now if you have ample storage space or copy just the end project file for each lesson as needed. Then you can delete it when you finish that lesson.

How to use the lessons

Each lesson in this book provides step-by-step instructions for creating one or more specific elements of a real-world project. Some lessons build on projects created in preceding lessons; most stand alone. All the lessons build on each other in terms of concepts and skills, so the best way to learn from this book is to proceed through the lessons in sequential order. In this book, some techniques and processes are explained and described in detail only the first few times you perform them.

The organization of the lessons is also project-oriented rather than feature-oriented. That means, for example, that you'll work with symbols on real-world design projects over several lessons rather than in just one chapter.

Additional resources

Adobe Edge Animate Classroom in a Book is not meant to replace documentation that comes with the program or to be a comprehensive reference for every feature. Only the commands and options used in the lessons are explained in this book. For comprehensive information about program features and tutorials, please refer to these resources:

Adobe Community Help: Community Help brings together active Adobe product users, Adobe product team members, authors, and experts to give you the most useful, relevant, and up-to-date information about Adobe products.

To access Community Help: To invoke Help, press F1 or choose Help > Edge Animate Help.

Adobe content is updated based on community feedback and contributions. You can add comments to both content or forums—including links to web content, publish your own content using Community Publishing, or contribute Cookbook Recipes. Find out how to contribute at www.adobe.com/community/publishing/download.html.

See http://community.adobe.com/help/profile/faq.html for answers to frequently asked questions about Community Help.

Adobe Edge Animate Help and Support: http://helpx.adobe.com/edge-animate/topics.html, where you can find and browse Help and Support content on adobe.com.

Adobe Forums: http://forums.adobe.com lets you tap into peer-to-peer discussions, questions, and answers on Adobe products.

Adobe TV: http://tv.adobe.com is an online video resource for expert instruction and inspiration about Adobe products, including a How To channel to get you started with your product.

Adobe Design Center: http://www.adobe.com/designcenter offers thoughtful articles on design and design issues, a gallery showcasing the work of top-notch designers, tutorials, and more.

Adobe Developer Connection: http://www.adobe.com/devnet is your source for technical articles, code samples, and how-to videos that cover Adobe developer products and technologies.

Resources for educators: http://www.adobe.com/education includes three free curriculums that use an integrated approach to teaching Adobe software and can be used to prepare for the Adobe Certified Associate exams.

Note: Many aspects of the Edge Animate application can be controlled by multiple techniques, such as a menu command, a button, dragging, and a keyboard shortcut. Only one or two of the methods are described in any given procedure so that you can learn different ways of working, even when the task is one you've done before.

Also check out these useful links:

Adobe Marketplace & Exchange: https://www.adobeexchange.com/ is a central resource for finding tools, services, extensions, code samples, and more to supplement and extend your Adobe products.

Adobe Edge Animate product home page: http://html.adobe.com/edge/animate/.

Adobe Labs: http://labs.adobe.com gives you access to early builds of cutting-edge technology, as well as forums where you can interact with both the Adobe development teams building that technology and other like-minded members of the community.

Adobe certification

The Adobe training and certification programs are designed to help Adobe customers improve and promote their product-proficiency skills. There are four levels of certification:

- Adobe Certified Associate (ACA)
- Adobe Certified Expert (ACE)
- Adobe Certified Instructor (ACI)
- Adobe Authorized Training Center (AATC)

The Adobe Certified Associate (ACA) credential certifies that individuals have the entry-level skills to plan, design, build, and maintain effective communications using different forms of digital media.

The Adobe Certified Expert program is a way for expert users to upgrade their credentials. You can use Adobe certification as a catalyst for getting a raise, finding a job, or promoting your expertise.

If you are an ACE-level instructor, the Adobe Certified Instructor program takes your skills to the next level and gives you access to a wide range of Adobe resources.

Adobe Authorized Training Centers offer instructor-led courses and training on Adobe products, employing only Adobe Certified Instructors. A directory of AATCs is available at http://partners.adobe.com.

For information on the Adobe Certified programs, visit http://www.adobe.com/support/certification/main.html.

1 GETTING STARTED

Lesson Overview

In this lesson, you'll learn how to do the following:

- Create a new composition in Edge Animate
- Save your Edge Animate composition
- Understand Edge Animate's file organization and the dependent files
- Adjust Stage settings and document properties
- Understand and manage your workspace
- Create simple elements
- Move and reposition elements on the Stage
- Organize overlapping elements
- Use the lock and hide options
- Add keyframes to create basic motion
- Move keyframes to change the pacing and timing
- Understand the playhead and the Timeline's playback functions
- Undo mistakes
- Preview your Edge Animate animation

 This lesson will take about one hour to complete. Open the Lesson01 folder from the *Adobe Edge Animate Classroom in a Book* lesson files to begin.

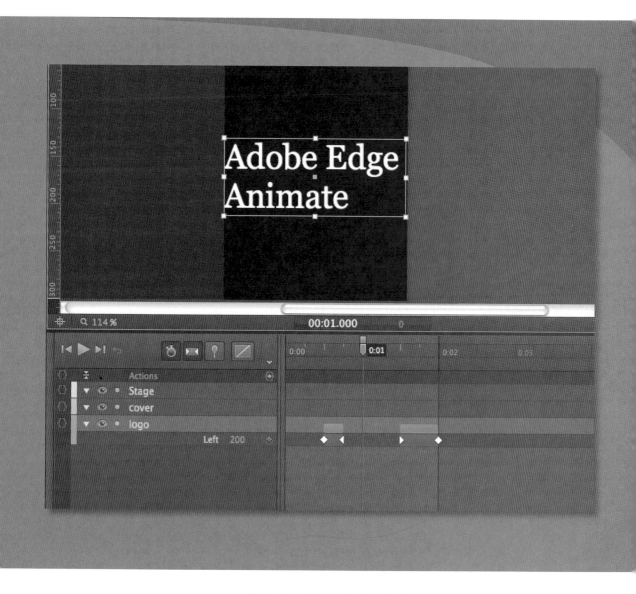

In Adobe Edge Animate, the Stage is where you organize the layout of your elements, and the Elements panel determines their overlapping order. The Timeline panel manages how those elements change over time for animation. Other panels let you edit and control your composition.

Starting Edge Animate

The first time you start Edge Animate you'll see a large Getting Started panel with links to tutorials, resources, and a list of recently opened files (which should be empty if you haven't yet opened a file). On the left side of the panel are buttons to open a file and create a new file. Adobe provides short in-app lessons, which are valuable for a quick run-through of Edge Animate's powerful features. It leads you step by step through some of the basic processes of creating animation and interactivity. Take some time to run through at least the first few lessons to get a leg up on understanding Edge Animate.

In this lesson, you'll create a simple logo animation with a box and some text to get a feel for the program. You'll create all the visual elements within Edge Animate, and in the process, you'll learn about positioning elements on the Stage and organizing them in the Elements panel. You'll also work with keyframes and the playhead to create basic motion in the Timeline.

It's important to understand that you'll use the Stage to organize your visual elements spatially, and you'll use the Timeline to organize your elements temporally. You'll learn to "read" the Timeline so you'll recognize how certain properties of your elements change through time.

1 Start Adobe Edge Animate. In Windows, choose Start > Programs > Adobe Edge Animate. In Mac OS, click Adobe Edge Animate in the Applications folder or the Dock.

2 Choose File > Open or click the Open File link from the Getting Started opening panel. In the Open dialog box, select the 01End.an file in the Lesson01/01End folder and click Open to see the final project.

3 Choose File > Preview in Browser.

Edge Animate creates the necessary files to display the final animation in your default browser, which opens automatically. A simple animation plays. During the animation, an Edge Animate logo emerges from behind a box, then exits to the right.

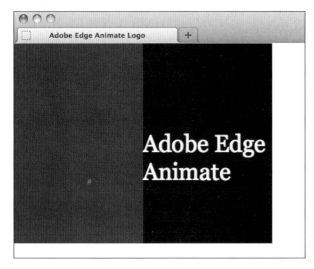

Note: You can also start Edge Animate by double-clicking an Edge Animate file (*.an), such as the 01End.an file that is provided, to show you the completed project.

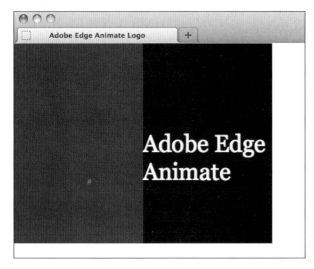

4 Close the browser.

Creating and saving a new composition

You'll create the simple animation that you just previewed by starting a new document. In Edge Animate, a new document is called a *composition*.

1   In Edge Animate, close the 01End file and choose File > New, or click the Create New link from the Getting Started panel.

Edge Animate creates a new untitled composition at the default settings of 550 pixels wide by 400 pixels high.

2   Choose File > Save. Name the file **01_workingcopy**, and from the Format pull-down menu, leave as Html file. Save it in the 01Start folder. Saving your composition right away is a good working habit and ensures your work won't be lost if the application or your computer crashes.

Your Edge Animate source file is saved as 01_workingcopy.an. Notice the other files that get saved along with your source file.

In addition to the source file, Edge Animate saves an HTML file, various JavaScript files (with the .js extension), and an additional folder of JavaScript files. The HTML file is your final published file that contains your Edge Animate composition. The JavaScript files provide the code that powers the animation and interactivity, and all the files are required to make your Edge Animate composition work. You'll learn more about publishing and publishing options in the last lesson in this book.

Note: Edge Animate adds an asterisk next to the filename above the Stage if there are any unsaved changes to your composition. Save your work, and the asterisk disappears.

Getting to know the workspace

The Adobe Edge Animate workspace includes the command menus at the top of the screen and a variety of tools and panels for editing and adding elements to your composition. You can create simple objects such as rectangles, rounded rectangles, ellipses, and text for your animation in Edge Animate. You can also import richer visual elements that you've created in Adobe Illustrator, Adobe Photoshop, and other applications that output compatible graphic formats. In the next lesson, you'll learn more about creating and importing artwork.

By default, Edge Animate displays the menu bar, the Tools panel at the top, the Properties panel on the left, the Timeline on the bottom, and the Elements, Library, and Lessons panels on the right. In the center, Edge Animate shows the current composition, which is the rendered HTML file. The white rectangular area is the Stage, which is displayed at the dimensions of the composition.

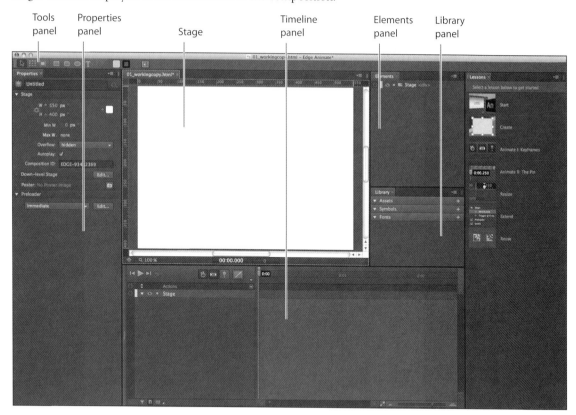

Note: As you work in Edge Animate, you can open, close, dock, undock, and move panels around the screen to fit your work style or your screen resolution. Use the options on the upper-right corner of the panel to dock or undock it. Choose Window > Workspace > New Workspace to save your custom arrangement of panels.

About the Stage

The big white rectangle in the middle of your screen is called the Stage. As with a theater stage, the Stage in Edge Animate is the area that viewers see when a movie is playing. It contains all the visual elements, such as text or images, that appear on the browser screen. Move elements on and off the Stage to move them in and out of view. You move objects manually with the Selection tool, or you can change their X or Y values in the Properties panel to position them precisely. Additionally, you can use the Modify > Align and Modify > Distribute commands to position multiple elements uniformly on the Stage. You'll learn more about the Align and Distribute commands in the later lessons of this book.

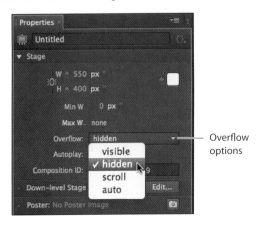

Overflow options

The Overflow option in the Properties panel determines how elements that are off the Stage appear. For now, keep the Overflow option at hidden to hide any element that is not on the Stage.

Zooming in or out of the Stage

To zoom in or out of the Stage, you can choose different magnifications from the top menu View options. To zoom in and see less of the Stage, press Ctrl and + (Windows)/Command and + (Mac OS). To zoom out and see more of the Stage, press Ctrl and – (Windows)/Command and – (Mac OS). Choose View > Actual Size or press Ctrl+1 (Windows)/Command+1 (Mac OS) to show the Stage at 100%. You can also change the zoom level by changing the magnification value at the bottom left of the Stage. Click the crosshairs icon to center the Stage.

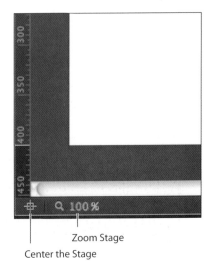

Zoom Stage

Center the Stage

Changing the Stage properties

Now, you'll change the color and dimensions of the Stage. The Stage color, dimensions, and other document properties are available in the Properties panel, which is the vertical panel just to the left of the Stage.

1 At the top of the Properties panel, note that the dimensions of the current Stage are set at 550 x 400 pixels.

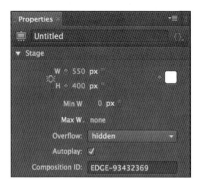

2 Click the chain icon connecting the W (width) and the H (height) properties under Stage if it isn't already broken.

The chain icon keeps the Stage dimensions proportional. Unlinking the chain lets you change the width and the height independently.

3 Choose 400 for the width and 300 for the height. Make sure that the units are in pixels (px) rather than percent. You'll learn more about using percent-based layouts for responsive design in the last lesson. You can also click and drag on the pixel values, and the Stage dimensions update in real time.

4 Click the white color chip to the right of the Stage dimensions to choose a new color from the Color picker.

5 Choose a new hue from the vertical rainbow and the saturation and brightness level from the color gamut. You also have the option of entering RGB and Alpha numeric values, or hexadecimal values. For this exercise, click on the black swatch at the top right of the Color picker.

Your Stage is now black and resized at 400 pixels by 300 pixels. You can change these Stage properties at any time.

Naming your composition

You've saved your Edge Animate composition, but you still need to give your composition an actual name. The name appears at the top of the browser window and is used for bookmarking and indexing purposes for search engines.

1 At the top of the Properties panel, replace Untitled with a name of your own choosing. Since you'll be creating an Adobe Edge Animate animated logo, you can enter **Adobe Edge Animate Logo**.

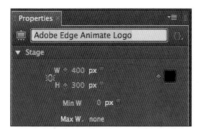

2 Press Enter (Windows) or Return (Mac OS) or click outside the field to finalize the name.

Working with elements

After setting up your Stage properties, you'll create the visual elements to animate. Adobe Edge Animate can display and animate a variety of graphics—from imported images such as PNG, JPEG, and other bitmap files, to scalable vector graphics (SVG files). You'll learn more about how to import and handle imported graphics in the next lesson. In this lesson, you'll create your own simple graphics within Edge Animate using the Rectangle and the Text tools.

Adding an element

An element is any object imported into or created within Edge Animate. Elements appear in the Elements panel as well as on the Timeline. Each element has a unique name so that Edge Animate (and other code) can identify the element for display, animation, or interactive purposes. For example, an imported JPEG, a piece of text, and a box created within Edge Animate are all elements. You can also create groupings and special objects called symbols, but they are also essentially elements (although slightly more complicated ones). Even a background image that remains constant throughout an animation is an element with a unique name.

The elements that you can create within Edge Animate are rectangles, rounded rectangles, ellipses, and text. Other shape variations are possible after rotating or skewing those elements. These elements are graphics that are native to the browser. The browser uses HTML to create the elements and CSS to style them.

1   Choose the Rectangle tool.

2   Click on the background color swatch to the right of the drawing tools.

The Color picker opens.

Note: You can disable the Smart Guides that appear on the Stage by toggling View > Enable Smart Guides or press Ctrl+; (Windows])/Ctrl+; (Mac OS).

3 Choose a deep red color for the background color of your rectangle.

4 Click outside the Color picker to close it.

5 Leave the border color at the default black.

6 Click on the top-left corner of the Stage and drag out a rectangle that covers the left side of the Stage. As you create your rectangle, notice how pink Smart Guides appear to help you align the rectangle to the Stage. Your rectangle will "snap" to the guides like a magnet does to metal.

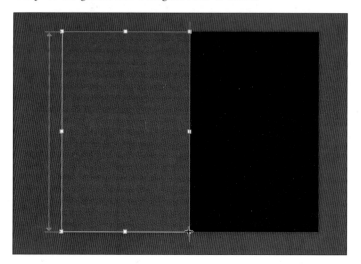

A red rectangle without a border appears on the left side of the Stage.

Notice that a new element called **Rectangle** appears in both your Elements panel and in the Timeline panel. The Elements panel shows that the element is a <div> tag, which is the way to mark up a unique piece of content in HTML.

Note: While rectangles, rounded rectangles, and ovals are created as <div> elements, text and images can be identified with different HTML tags such as <img> or <p>, <h1>, <h2>, and so on. Those different tag options are available for text and images at the top of the Properties panel next to the element's name.

Positioning an element

If your rectangle isn't positioned precisely at the edges of the Stage at the time you create it, don't worry, because you can always move your elements.

1   Choose the Selection tool, and click on your rectangle on the Stage.

2   Drag the rectangle around the Stage.

Notice how the X and Y values under Position and Size in the Properties panel change as you drag the rectangle to new positions on the Stage.

3   Position the rectangle so the X value is at 0 and the Y value is at 0. You can also click and drag the X and Y values themselves in the Properties panel, or simply enter new values for X and Y from the keyboard.

In general, Edge Animate measures browser coordinates with the origin at the top-left corner. So, X=0 corresponds to the left edge of the Stage, with X values increasing to the right. Y=0 corresponds to the top edge of the Stage, with Y values increasing to the bottom.

Note: The coordinate system and an object's reference point can become more complicated when you start dealing with responsive design, which you'll learn about in the last lesson in this book. The Global, Applied, and coordinate picker options in the Properties panel allow relative positioning of objects rather than fixed pixel positioning.

Modifying the size of an element

All the properties listed in the Properties panel can be changed. Follow these steps to change the size of your rectangle:

1   Select your rectangle element on the Stage.

2   Under Position and Size in the Properties panel, click the chain link icon between W and H to break it, if it's not already broken.

The broken chain link allows you to change the width and height of your rectangle independently. Click the icon again to restore the chain link, and the width and height will be linked to change proportionally.

3 Modify the W and H values so the width is 200 pixels and the height is 300 pixels.

Your rectangle should now be exactly half the size of the Stage and positioned flush against the top and left edges.

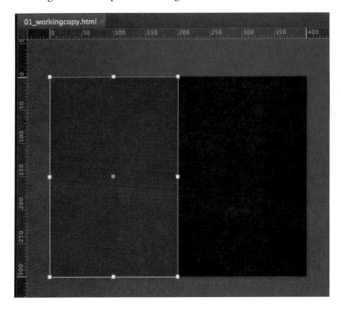

Renaming an element

It's a good practice to maintain a consistent naming practice, not only for file and folder names on your computer, but for the elements on your Stage as well. For complex projects, you'll likely be dealing with dozens or more elements. Giving them intuitive names will help you maintain order now and avoid headaches later.

1 In the Elements panel or in the Timeline panel, double-click the default name of your element, Rectangle.

The name becomes highlighted, allowing you to edit it.

2 Replace the name Rectangle with the name **cover**.

In this simple animation, an Adobe Edge Animate logo will emerge from under the red rectangle, so the name "cover" is a logical choice. The new name updates in the Elements panel, the Timeline panel, and in the Properties panel.

3 Alternately, you can rename your element in the ID field at the top of the Properties panel.

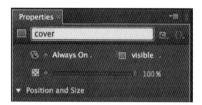

Naming your elements

The name of your HTML element is its unique ID attribute. There are a few rules to follow when you rename your elements:

- Names must begin with a letter or an underscore
- Names can be any combination of letters, numbers, hyphens, or underscores
- Names are case-sensitive
- You cannot have more than one element with the same name

Fortunately, Edge Animate is smart enough to warn you of any incompatible names. If you try to name an element that doesn't conform to these rules, Edge Animate displays a yellow warning sign next to your

name and modifies it so it is acceptable. If you try to give a duplicate name to an element, Edge Animate will simply not accept it.

Creating text

Now it's time to add the logo. You'll create it with the Text tool.

1 Choose the Text tool in the Tools panel above the Properties panel.

2 Click on the Stage to place the initial text insertion point.

A text-editing box appears.

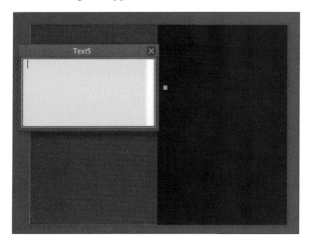

3 Enter **Adobe Edge Animate** as the text and press the Escape key or click outside the text-editing box to exit the Text tool.

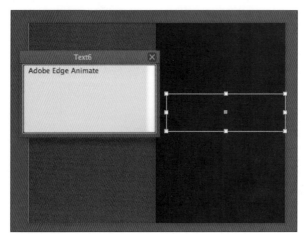

Your text appears on the Stage, and a new `<div>` element is added in the Elements and Timeline panels.

You may not be able to see your text on the Stage, however, if the color of the text is the same color as the background.

4 While the text is still selected, click the color swatch in the Text section of the Properties panel.

The Color picker opens.

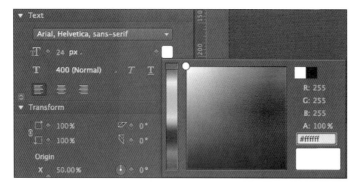

5 Choose white for the text color.

6 Click outside the Color picker to close it.

The color of your text changes to white.

7 While the text is still selected, choose Georgia for the font and 36 pixels for the font size. Position the text at the left edge of the Stage and centered vertically so X=0 and Y=109. Set the width property (W) to 200.

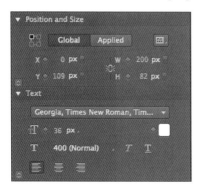

UNIVERSITY OF WINCHESTER
LIBRARY

8 Rename your newly created element **logo**.

● **Note:** If you make a mistake in creating one of your elements, and wish to start over, you can easily delete any element by selecting it on the Stage or the Elements panel, and pressing the Delete key.

Your text appears on the left side of the Stage, centered vertically on the Stage.

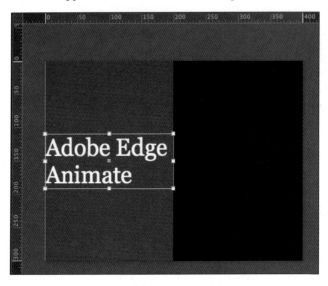

Managing overlapping elements

Your current composition contains two elements: a rectangle and some text. The text, which was created most recently, lies on top of the rectangle. Since you'll want the Adobe Edge Animate logo to emerge from under the rectangle, you need to arrange the elements so the text is behind the rectangle.

The Elements panel allows you to manage how elements overlap each other.

1 The Elements panel contains three items: a Stage element, which represents the main Stage on which you are placing your other elements; the element you named logo; and the element you named cover.

The logo and cover elements are indented under the Stage element. This represents a parent-child hierarchy: the Stage is the parent and the elements under it are the children. Your Edge Animate composition

will always be identified by the Stage `<div>` in the final HTML document, and therefore, you can't rename your Stage.

Under the Stage element, the logo element is *above* the cover element. Elements that are on top of the stack in the Elements panel overlap the elements that are lower in the stack.

2 Drag the logo element and drop it *under* the cover element.

A bold black line indicates the destination of your rearrangement. The logo now becomes covered by the cover element on the Stage.

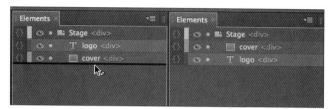

Note: Make sure you move your logo element under your cover element, and not on top of it—if that happens, you'll create a parent-child relationship for your elements. Simply drag your logo element back to its correct position, if needed.

The order of elements on the Timeline is also updated to show the cover on top and the logo underneath. On your Stage, the text is no longer visible because it is under the red rectangle.

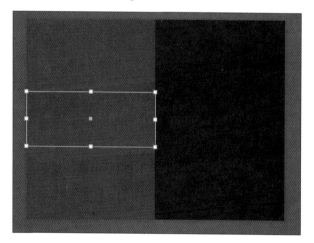

Note: You can also arrange elements by choosing Modify > Arrange from the menu at the top of the interface. Use Bring to Front or Send to Back to move a selected element to the top or bottom of the stack. Use Bring Forward or Send Backward to move a selected element just one layer up or down in the stack.

Understanding the Element and Timeline panels

The Element and Timeline panels organize your entire Edge Animate composition, so knowing how to "read" them is essential to your success in creating compelling animations and interactive projects.

You've already seen how the Elements panel displays element hierarchies and shows how elements overlap each other. The Elements panel also displays the names (unique div IDs) for each element, which can be changed at any time.

The Timeline panel parallels the Elements panel by showing similar, but not identical information. In the Elements panel, the elements show their hierarchy. The cover and logo elements, for example, are child elements of the Stage, and are indented. In the Timeline panel, however, a triangle hides or shows the properties for each Element that change in an animation. Notice that in the Timeline, each element (the Stage, cover, and logo) has its own triangle.

Expanding the triangle by clicking on them doesn't reveal additional information because you haven't yet inserted any animation.

Later in this lesson, when you begin to animate the logo, you'll see that the Timeline panel keeps track of how each property of an element changes through time.

The Elements, Timeline, and Stage work together in other respects. Selecting an element in one panel, for example, highlights that element in all of the other panels. Each element is also color-coded between the Elements and Timeline panels.

Using the Lock and Visibility options

Your logo currently sits below the cover, which makes it difficult to select to edit or move. You can use the Lock and Visibility options in the Elements and Timeline panels to fix or hide certain elements in order to focus on others.

1   In the Elements or the Timeline panel, click the Visibility option (eye icon) next to the cover element.

The eye icon turns into a white dot, indicating that the cover element is currently not visible.

The rectangle on the Stage disappears, revealing the text that sits behind it.

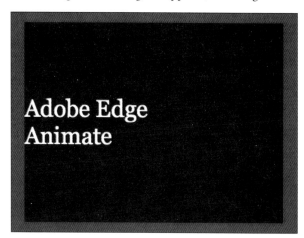

Note: Don't mistake the Visibility option in the Timeline and Elements panel with the Display property in the Properties panel. The Display property determines whether or not an element is displayed in the browser. You use the Display property to make an element suddenly appear or disappear from the Stage during an animation. The Visibility option is purely an interface feature within Edge Animate that helps you work with multiple elements.

Note: Lock or hide multiple elements at once by Shift-selecting multiple items. Hold down the Shift key and click on your elements in the Elements or Timeline panel. You can also click and drag through multiple elements to lock or hide them quickly. To select non-contiguous elements, hold down the Ctrl/Command key. With multiple elements selected, right-click and choose Lock or Hide from the contextual menu that appears.

2   Click on the Visibility option for the cover element to make it visible again.

3   Click on the white dot next to the Visibility option for the cover element.

The white dot turns into a lock symbol, indicating that the logo element is currently locked and cannot be moved or edited. Use the lock option to fix individual elements so you don't accidentally move them, and they still remain visible.

Note: When you lock or hide an element in one panel (the Stage, the Elements panel, or the Timeline panel), it is locked or hidden in the others.

Adding motion

It's time to add motion to your composition so your Adobe Edge Animate logo can make its dramatic appearance. You'll animate the text moving from left to right, and in doing so, you'll learn about properties, keyframes, timing, and pacing. You'll learn to use the playhead and get comfortable with the Timeline panel. We'll go into much further detail in later lessons, so we'll focus on the basics first.

About Animation

Quite simply, animation is the change of a property over time. Motion is the change of location over time—if an object starts at one position and ends at another, then you have an object that moves. Your job as the animator is to tell Edge Animate where the object is at the start and where the object is at the end. Edge Animate will fill in the intervening space between the start and end times to create a smooth animation. The key points in time (the start and end times) when an object has different properties are called *keyframes*.

A keyframe is a common concept among animators. In video-editing software, 3D animation software, and even in traditional hand-drawn animation, keyframes refer to those points along a timeline when there is a change in the object or character.

Edge Animate has several different ways to help you animate with keyframes. We'll start with a basic approach of defining both the starting and ending keyframes in separate steps.

Inserting the beginning keyframe

Your goal is to animate the logo moving from its current position to a position to the right. So the first task is to establish the starting keyframe at its current position.

1 Make sure the cover element is locked or hidden, and the logo element is unlocked so you can manipulate the logo without disturbing the rectangle.

2 Select the logo element in the Elements panel or Timeline.

3 The playhead, which is the downward-pointing marker at the top of the Timeline with the vertical red line, indicates the current time. The playhead should be at the start of the Timeline, or 0:00 seconds.

4 In the Properties panel, click the Add Keyframe button (empty diamond icon) in front of the X property.

Edge Animate inserts a keyframe for its horizontal property of the logo element at the current location of the playhead (0:00 seconds). In the Timeline, a new lane under the logo element appears with the horizontal property keyframe labeled as Left. The property is labeled Left because its left edge is being used as the point of reference.

Using Auto-Keyframe and Auto-Transition modes

Now that you've established the keyframe for the beginning position, it's time to create the keyframe for the ending position. Fortunately, you don't have to manually create keyframes each time you want the logo to move to a new position. Edge Animate provides an easy approach called Auto-Keyframe and Auto-Transition modes, which are both turned on by default.

Auto-Keyframe mode is indicated by the stopwatch icon in the Timeline panel. When Auto-Keyframe mode is on, the stopwatch is red and appears depressed. When Auto-Keyframe mode is off, the stopwatch is gray and appears raised. Auto-Transition mode is indicated by the green-colored bar between two half-diamonds. It turns gray when disabled.

Auto-Keyframe mode (on)
Auto-Transition mode (on)

With auto-keyframing, Edge Animate automatically inserts a keyframe whenever you make a change to an element along the Timeline. Auto-Transition creates the smooth transitions between keyframes.

1 Move the playhead by dragging it to the 0:00.500 mark, which represents 0.5 seconds. You can also simply click on the top of the Timeline panel to move the playhead, or use the time counter to enter the exact numeric value.

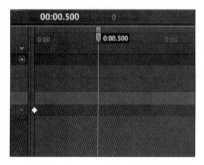

● **Note:** As you drag the playhead along the Timeline, it will snap to major time markers and keyframes. You can turn the snapping behavior on or off by toggling the Timeline Snapping option at the bottom of the Timeline panel.

2 Select the logo element.

3 Holding the Shift key, drag the logo element to the right on the Stage until its left edge aligns with the right edge of the cover element. The X value for the logo element should be X=200 pixels.

Holding the Shift key constrains the positioning of objects at right angles. A green line indicates that the logo is constrained along the horizontal axis.

A new keyframe, indicated by a white diamond, is inserted at the 0:00.500-second mark in the lane labeled Left (which refers to the left edge of the text element). A colored track between the beginning and ending keyframes represents an animation: the values of the X property change from the first keyframe to the next. Congratulations, you've just created your first motion!

4   Grab the playhead and drag it back and forth between the two keyframes on the Timeline panel. The back-and-forth dragging motion of the playhead is called *scrubbing*.

As you scrub, the logo on the Stage moves from its initial position to its final position on the right. You can also see the value of its horizontal position in the Timeline change between 0 and 0.5 seconds.

Previewing the motion

While scrubbing is an effective way to view the motion while under your control, you should preview your composition to get a sense of how the animation would appear to your audience running at normal speed.

Previewing within Edge Animate

Use the playback controls at the top-left side of the Timeline panel to play back your animation.

Go to Start
Play
Go to End
Return to Last Play Position

- Click the Play button (triangular icon).

   Edge Animate plays your animation from the current position of the playhead. The playhead moves across the Timeline from left to right, displaying the changing properties of the elements on the Stage. When the playhead reaches the end of the Timeline, it stops.

- Click the Stop button while the playhead is moving to stop playback.

- Alternately, press the spacebar to play or stop the playhead.

- Click the Go to End button to move the playhead to the end of the Timeline.

- Click the Go to Start button to move the playhead to the start of the Timeline.

- If you want to review just a portion of your animation on the Timeline, you can click the Return to Last Play Position button.

   Edge Animate moves the playhead to its last position on the Timeline, so you can play the animation from that point again easily.

Previewing in the browser

It's also a good idea to preview your animation in its ultimate playback environment—a browser—to see how all your elements are coming together. When you preview your composition in a browser, elements that may have been hidden with the Visibility option are shown normally.

1   Choose File > Preview in Browser, or Ctrl+Enter (Windows) or Command+Return (Mac OS).

Edge Animate updates the HTML file and all the necessary dependent CSS and JavaScript files and opens your default browser. Your browser displays and plays your animation of the Adobe Edge Animate logo moving out from under the red rectangular cover.

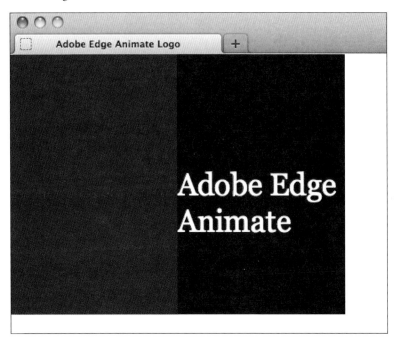

2   Click the Refresh button on your browser.

The browser reloads the Edge Animate file and replays your animation.

Continuing and modifying the motion

Next, you'll add another motion for the logo to make its exit. The logo will remain on the Stage for just a second so the audience can read it, and then quickly move off the Stage to the right. The additional motion requires a few more keyframes, which you'll add in the following steps.

Inserting additional keyframes

Earlier in this lesson, you added keyframes from the Properties panel. You can also add keyframes to existing properties from the Timeline.

1 Move the playhead to the 0:01.500-second mark on the Timeline.

You want your logo to stay in its current position for 1 second after it emerges from under the cover, so you need to insert a keyframe at 1.5 seconds to establish the beginning of its next motion.

Note: You can also insert a keyframe by clicking the Add Keyframe icon for the X property in the Properties panel.

2 Click the Add Keyframe button (diamond icon) in the Left lane of the Timeline panel.

Note: Another way to insert keyframes is to right-click on the Timeline and choose Add Keyframe, or choose Timeline > Add Keyframe and add a keyframe for the property of your choice.

Edge Animate inserts a keyframe for the X property at 0:01.500 seconds.

3 Move the playhead to the 0:02-second mark on the Timeline.

The 0:02-second mark will be the end of the animation.

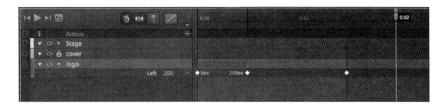

4 Make sure that Auto-Keyframe and Auto-Transition modes are enabled. Holding the Shift key, drag the logo to the right off the Stage. The X property of the logo should be at 400 pixels.

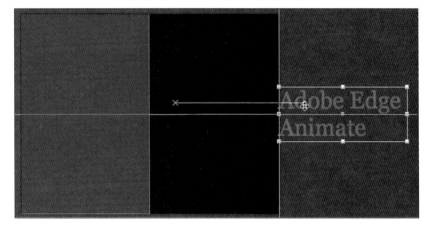

Edge Animate automatically inserts a keyframe for the new X property at 0:02 seconds, and a second colored bar in the Left lane appears, indicating that there is another animation between the two keyframes from 0:01.500 to 0:02 seconds.

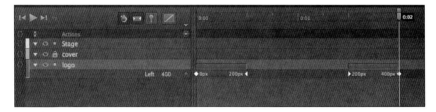

5 Press the spacebar to preview your motion.

The Adobe Edge Animate logo moves from 0:00 to 0:00.500 seconds, then stops. At 0:01.500 seconds, it moves again and exits the Stage to the right.

Deleting keyframes and properties

If you've accidentally added keyframes for unnecessary properties, you can always remove them easily.

1 Select your logo element and click the Add Keyframe icon for its Y property in the Properties panel, as an example of a mistake.

Edge Animate creates a keyframe for the logo element's vertical position, and a new lane labeled Top appears in the Timeline.

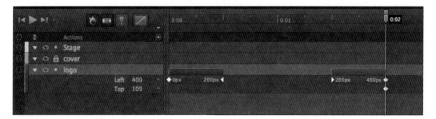

2 Assuming that the keyframe for the Y property is a mistake, select the property lane in the Timeline.

The keyframe is highlighted, indicating that is selected.

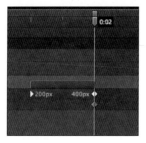

3 Press the delete key.

Edge Animate deletes the keyframe. Since there is only one keyframe in that property lane, the entire lane from the Timeline panel is deleted.

Moving keyframes to change pacing

The position of keyframes on the Timeline determines how quickly or slowly an animation proceeds. If the start and end keyframes of a motion are close together, then the animation takes place in a much shorter time frame, and the result is a quicker motion. If the start and end keyframes of a motion are far apart, then the animation has more time, and the result is a slower motion.

Edit the position of any of your keyframes simply by dragging them along the Timeline.

1 Move your cursor over the end keyframe of the first animation span.

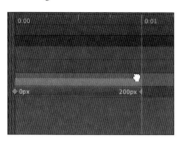

Your cursor changes to a double-headed arrow, indicating that you can move the end of the animation (its last keyframe).

2 Click and drag the keyframe to 0:01 second.

The length of the first motion becomes longer.

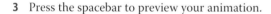

3 Press the spacebar to preview your animation.

The Adobe Edge Animate logo now takes twice as long to emerge from under the rectangular cover, and it remains on the Stage for only .5 seconds.

4 Click and drag the last keyframe of the first animation span to 0:00.250 seconds.

The length of the first motion becomes shorter.

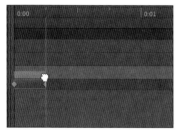

5 Press the spacebar to preview your animation.

The Adobe Edge Animate logo now takes only half as long to emerge from under the rectangular cover, but remains on the Stage for a much longer time.

Moving keyframes to change timing

In addition to moving individual keyframes to lengthen or shorten an animation, you can move both keyframes that bracket an animation to change the timing of when it happens.

1 Select the first animation span by clicking
   on the colored bar between its keyframes.

   Edge Animate highlights the keyframes
   and the animation span.

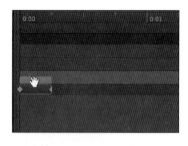

2 Move your cursor over the animation
   span.

   Your cursor changes to a hand, indicating
   that you can move the animation.

3 Click and drag the animation so it begins
   at 0:00.500 seconds.

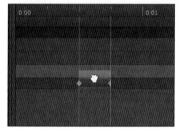

4 Press the spacebar to preview your
   animation.

   There is now a slight pause in your
   composition before the Adobe Edge
   Animate logo quickly darts out from
   under the rectangular cover. It remains on
   the Stage briefly before slowly making its exit to the right.

   Pacing and timing are important in animation to create variety, tension, and
   drama. Explore different ways in which the logo can move by experimenting
   with the position of keyframes on the Timeline.

Undoing mistakes

In a perfect world, everything would go according to plan. But sometimes you
need to move back a step or two and start over. You can undo steps in Edge
Animate just as you do in other programs, using the Undo command.

To undo a single step in Edge Animate, choose Edit > Undo or press Ctrl+Z
(Windows) or Command+Z (Mac OS). To redo a step you've undone, choose Edit >
Redo or Shift+Ctrl+Z (Windows) or Shift+Command+Z (Mac OS).

Next steps

You've made it! You've successfully created your own graphics and set them in
motion. You've explored the Edge Animate workspace and are more comfortable
with the terminology and working process. You're ready to dig deeper to master
the details of this groundbreaking new motion and interactive design tool. In the
following lessons, you'll learn more about graphics, animation, interactivity, and
integrating rich media. Onward!

Review questions

1 How do you manage overlapping elements?

2 How do you manually add a keyframe?

3 What are the rules for acceptable names for elements?

4 What is Auto-Keyframe mode?

5 How do you lock or hide an element?

Review answers

1 You can manage overlapping elements by dragging the elements in the Elements panel to a new position in the stack. Elements that are higher in the panel overlap those that are lower in the panel. You can also select an element and choose Modify > Arrange from the top menu to change the overlapping order of elements.

2 Add a keyframe by clicking the Add Keyframe button in front of a property in the Properties panel, or by clicking the Add Keyframe button in a Property lane of the Timeline panel. You can also right-click on the Timeline and choose Add Keyframe from the contextual menu, or choose Timeline > Add Keyframe.

3 Names of elements must begin with a letter or an underscore, must contain only numbers, letters, hyphens, or underscores, and must be unique.

4 Auto-Keyframe mode is enabled when the stopwatch icon in the Timeline panel is red and appears depressed. Auto-Keyframe mode automatically inserts the appropriate property keyframes when you modify your object on the Stage.

5 Hide an element by clicking the Visibility option in the Elements or Timeline panel. Lock an element by clicking on the Lock option in the Elements or Timeline panel. You can also select an element and right-click and choose Lock or Hide from the contextual menu.

2 CREATING GRAPHICS AND IMPORTING ART

Lesson Overview

In this lesson, you'll learn how to do the following:

- Work with different graphic file formats
- Import artwork
- Understand the Library panel
- Create and modify rectangles
- Resize and rotate elements
- Align and distribute multiple elements
- Change an element's center of rotation and transformation
- Use Smart Guides
- Constrain sizing and positioning
- Use the Transform tool
- Understand element hierarchy and inheritance
- Add drop shadows
- Create and edit text
- Add web fonts for expressive typography
- Understand fallback fonts

 This lesson will take about an hour to complete. Open the Lesson02 folder from the *Adobe Edge Animate Classroom in a Book* lesson files to begin.

Creating, importing, and managing graphics is the first step in making a splash with Edge Animate. Learn to work with a variety of imported graphic files and native HTML elements. (Logo by LogoOpenStock.com)

Lesson overview

In this lesson, you'll explore the various ways to get stunning visuals into an Edge Animate composition. You'll import various types of images as well as create and modify graphics directly within Edge Animate. You'll create a fictional advertisement for a local cafe for its new fall drink specials. Since this lesson focuses on understanding graphics, the composition will be mostly static, with just a small amount of motion at the end to make it a little more interesting.

1   Choose File > Open or click the Open File link from the Getting Started opening panel. In the Open dialog box, select the 02End.an file in the Lesson02/02End folder and click Open to see the final project.

2   Choose File > Preview in Browser, or press Ctrl+Enter (Windows)/ Command+Return (Mac OS).

Edge Animate creates the necessary files to display the final animation in your default browser, which opens automatically. The browser shows a richly layered advertisement consisting of a background image of fall foliage, layered semi-transparent colored shapes, some descriptive text, and a company logo. A leaf slowly rocks back and forth in one of the corners.

3   Close the browser.

4   In Edge Animate, choose File > New, or press Ctrl+N (Windows)/Command+N (Mac OS) to start a new document.

5   In the Properties panel, change the Stage size to 640 pixels wide and 420 pixels high. Choose a brown color (#7d4d15) for the background color of the Stage.

6   In the Properties panel, enter **Mucho Gusto Café** as the name of the composition.

7   Save your file as **02_workingcopy** in the 02Start folder.

Understanding graphic formats

Adobe Edge Animate is not a program for drawing like other animation or graphic processing tools. Unlike Adobe Illustrator, Edge Animate has no capabilities to create free-form shapes. And unlike Adobe Photoshop, Edge Animate has no ability to apply filters, color blending, or edit bitmap-based renderings.

Instead, Edge Animate uses HTML to identify objects in the browser and enlists CSS to style those objects. The CSS styling can be as simple as specifying an element's dimensions (its width and height) and color, or it can be as complex as changing an element's rotation, corner radius, amount of skew, or even applying a drop shadow. You can get a surprising variety of shapes from just the CSS styling of a basic rectangle.

As a common practice, you'll import the graphics that were created in other programs. Edge Animate can import these types of graphic file formats: PNG, JPEG, GIF, and SVG. The PNG, JPEG, and GIF file formats are bitmap graphics, which means that the images are described by pixels and can be modified by a bitmap-editing application such as Photoshop. An SVG (Scalable Vector Graphics) file supports vector graphics, which are drawings that are not described by pixels, but by curves, lines, and shapes.

Working with bitmaps

In this lesson, you've been provided with bitmap graphics so you can create the advertisement for the café's fall promotion. You'll begin by importing a JPEG of the background image and a PNG of a single leaf.

Importing the background image

When you import images into Edge Animate, the references to the files are stored in the Library panel. The images aren't actually saved inside your composition, as all assets remain external to your HTML document.

1 Choose File > Import, or press Ctrl+I (Windows)/Command+I (Mac OS), or click the Add Asset button on the right side of the Assets section of the Library panel.

The Import dialog box appears.

Note: Hold down the Shift key to select multiple files to import, or the Ctrl key (Windows) or Command key (Mac OS) to select multiple non-contiguous files.

2 Navigate to the graphics folder in the 02Start folder and select the fallbackground.jpg file.

3 Click Open.

Edge Animate imports the fallbackground.jpg file into your composition. The imported file appears in your Library panel, and on the Stage, if you've imported the file from the top menu.

The image file appears in the subdirectory called **graphics**, reflecting the relative path to the file from the Edge Animate source file.

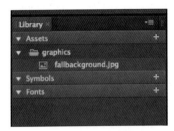

4 Select the image on the Stage. Drag the image from the Library panel to the Stage, if it isn't yet on the Stage.

In the Image section of the Properties panel, Edge Animate displays the same path information for the selected file.

The imported image file also appears and is automatically named in the Elements panel and in the Timeline panel.

5 Position the background image so X=0 and Y=0.

The background image covers the entire Stage.

Note: If you delete the image file from your Stage, the reference in the Library remains. To add it back to your composition, simply drag the file from the Library panel to the Stage.

Note: You can also import an image file into Edge Animate by dragging it from your desktop onto the Stage. Edge Animate displays the registration point and the values of the x- and y-coordinates for you to place the file in its desired position.

Understanding the Library panel

The Library panel organizes three important items: Assets, Symbols, and Fonts. *Assets* are the graphic files that you import into your composition. *Symbols* are objects unique to Edge Animate that allow you to create nested, independent animations. You'll learn about Symbols in Lesson 4. *Fonts* organize your custom Web fonts, which you will create later in this lesson.

Your image files in the Assets folder are not stored inside your Edge Animate composition, but merely show their locations relative to the Edge Animate document. You can quickly see where your files are located by right-clicking on a selection and choosing Reveal in Explorer (Windows) or Finder (Mac OS).

By default, Edge Animate looks for a folder called "images." If you already have an images folder that contains image files, then Edge Animate displays them without you having to use the Import command.

Unfortunately, you can't import images that are outside the directory of your Edge Animate composition. For example, you can't choose File > Import and browse for an image anywhere on your computer's hard drive. The image must be located in the same folder as your Edge Animate composition, or in a subfolder.

Modifying the opacity

You can modify the opacity of any element on the Stage. Different opacities can create a more layered, richer visual presentation.

1   Select the background image on the Stage, Timeline, or Elements panel.

2   In the Properties panel, drag the Opacity slider to the 60% position. Alternatively, you can click and drag the percentage value or double-click to enter the value directly from your keyboard.

The opacity of the background image decreases, allowing more of the brown color of the Stage to show through.

Importing the leaf

The leaf is a PNG-24 image file, which supports transparencies, known as an alpha channel. In the provided PNG file, the background is totally transparent so the leaf can blend in seamlessly with the JPEG background of the fall foliage.

1   Using the approach described in the previous section, import the leaf.png file from the graphics folder in the Start02 folder.

The leaf.png file appears on the Stage and in the graphics folder of the Library panel. The leaf element also appears in the Elements panel and in the Timeline panel.

2 Move the leaf element on the Stage so it is positioned at X = 43 and Y = −12.

You'll make further adjustments to the position and the rotation of the leaf after some of the other graphic elements are put in place. Use PNG images to build complex integrated scenes with multiple elements.

Working with vector graphics

Vector graphics, unlike their bitmap counterparts, are resolution-independent, so they can be enlarged without losing quality. If you were to enlarge the PNG image of the leaf that you just imported, you would see pixelation as it gets bigger because the number of pixels that make up the image is fixed.

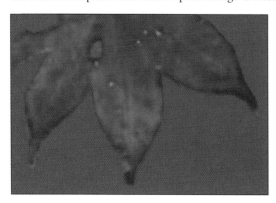

For images that need to be scaled up without losing quality, use the SVG format for vector graphics. In this section, you'll import SVG graphics of the café logo.

Importing vector graphics

The logo was created in Adobe Illustrator and saved as an SVG file. This logo template was originally created by LogoOpenStock.com for use under the Creative Commons license.

1   Choose File > Import or press Ctrl+I (Windows)/Command+I (Mac OS), or click the Add Asset button on the right side of the Assets section of the Library panel.

    The Import dialog box appears.

2   Navigate to the graphics folder in the 02Start folder and select the logo.svg file.

3   Click Open.

    Edge Animate imports the selected SVG file into your composition. The logo appears at the top-left corner of the Stage and the files appear in the Library panel within the graphics folder.

The SVG file is indicated by a different icon from the bitmap files, which will immediately help you differentiate the graphic formats of your imported assets.

Resizing elements

Now you'll resize the logo to fit the space for the ad. Since the logo is a vector graphic, you can play with the scaling until you're satisfied with your composition, and you won't have to worry about the loss of any image quality.

1 Select the logo element on the Stage or in the Elements or Timeline panel.

2 In the Properties panel, make sure that the Link Width and Height option is enabled, which links the W and H properties.

   The Link Width and Height icon should appear as an intact chain link.

3 Change the value of the width (W) property to 450 pixels, or the height (H) property to 200 pixels. You can either double-click the value and enter the number directly, or you can click and drag over the value to see the logo change scale gradually.

   The logo becomes enlarged proportionally in both dimensions.

4 Alternately, select the logo on the Stage with the Selection tool.

   A blue bounding box with control points appears around the selected element.

5 Move your cursor over a corner point of one of the bounding boxes until your cursor changes to a double-headed arrow.

6   Hold down the Shift key and click and drag the bounding box on the Stage.

The logo scales up and down freely. You can also see the changing values for the W and H properties in the Properties panel. Holding down the Shift key constrains the proportions of the resizing.

7   Position the logo at X=113 and Y=10.

●**Note:** When scaling SVG images, modify the Width and Height properties. If you scale SVG images by changing the Transform properties or with the Transform tool, the vector graphics will not maintain resolution independence and will show up pixelated on the Stage and in the browser.

Creating HTML elements

If you do not import graphic files into your composition, you'll be restricted to three visual elements that you can create directly in Edge Animate: rectangles, ellipses, and text. Rectangles, ellipses, and text can be modified with CSS, and with some creativity, you can create quite a few variations to use as buttons, background shapes, or design elements.

Creating a rectangle

Next, you'll create the elegant teardrop-shaped graphics that provide the background for the text. You'll start by creating a simple rectangle.

1   In the Tools panel, select the Rectangle tool (M).

2   Click the Background color swatch and choose a mustard-brown color (#786445) and change the Alpha value (opacity) to 80%. Leave the Border color as black.

3 Click and drag out a small rectangle on the Stage.

A small rectangle with a transparent brown background color and no border appears on the Stage.

4 In the Properties panel, make sure that the Link Width and Height icon is broken, and modify the W and H properties so the width is 180 pixels and the height is 120 pixels.

Modifying rectangles

While rectangles are useful for compartmentalizing your layout, you'll want to make these rectangles a little fancier for this advertisement. You'll round the corners and give it a slight angle and tilt.

Making rounded corners

Rounded corners can be applied to one, two, three, or all four corners of your rectangle. You control the amount of curvature by changing the pixel radius of each corner in the Properties panel or with the Transform tool.

1 Select the Transform tool (Q) in the Tools panel.

2 Click on the rectangle on the Stage.

A dark bounding box with black control points appears around the selected element.

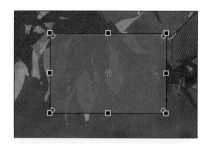

3 Move your cursor near the inside corner of the rectangle, just over the small black control point.

Your cursor should become an arrow.

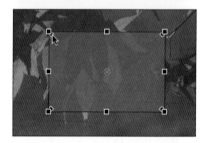

4 Click on the control point and drag it inward toward the center of the rectangle.

As you drag the control point toward the center, the corners of the rectangle become rounded. All four corners change with the same amount of curvature.

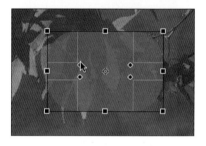

Click the triangle to expand the Corners section in the Properties panel. The amount of curvature is displayed as pixel units next to the corner radii diagram.

5 Move the control point in a diagonal direction away from the corner.

The corner curvature is constrained to an arc of a perfect circle. If you move the control point away from the diagonal, you can create curved corners that are elliptical in form.

6 Make the corners of the rectangle rounded with a 50-pixel radii. You can use the Transform tool or simply change the radius value in the Properties panel.

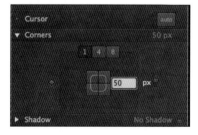

Creating asymmetric rounded corners

The rounded rectangle has more elegance, but what you really want is a shape that is more suggestive of a leaf, so you'll keep two opposite corners at right angles. The Properties panel has options that let you control the individual radii of each corner separately.

1   With the rounded rectangle selected, click on the top-left and bottom-right corners of the border radii diagram in the Properties panel.

The diagram indicates which corners can be modified, and which corners are locked. The modified corners are curved and raised; the unmodified corners appear with right angles and are depressed.

The top-left and bottom-right corners of your rounded rectangle on the Stage reset to right angles.

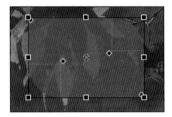

Note: The numeric buttons above the Border Radii diagram (1, 4, and 8) refer to the amount of control you can have over the symmetry of the rounded rectangle. When the 1 button is selected, a single value controls the radii of all four corners. When the 4 button is selected, each corner can have a different value. When the 8 button is selected, each corner can have two values for elliptical curvatures.

Note: The border radii values cannot be negative.

2   Continue to drag the inside-corner control points on the Transform bounding box around the rectangle on the Stage.

Notice that the curvature control points of the top-left and bottom-right corners have been reset.

Note: The control points for the border radii can actually be moved outside the bounds of the rectangle itself for severe curvatures.

Skewing the rectangle

The Transform tool appears in the Tools panel above the Properties panel. In addition to changing corner radii of rectangles, the Transform tool can change the rotation, scale, and skew of any element.

1   Select the rounded rectangle element on the Stage.

2   Choose the Transform tool from the Tools panel above the Properties panel.

A dark bounding box with black control points appears around the selected element.

3 Move your cursor close to the top or bottom horizontal edge of the bounding box.

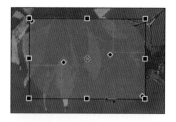

Your cursor turns into an icon of two arrows sliding past each other, indicating that you can skew the selection.

Note: Edge Animate only allows skew values between –90 to 90 degrees. Although smaller or larger values are accepted in the skewX or skewY CSS properties, those values cause the object to flip.

4 Click and drag the selection to the right or left.

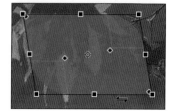

The rounded rectangle tilts slightly and the value of the skewX property in the Transform section of the Properties inspector changes. Tilt the rectangle until the skewX value is about 10 degrees.

Using the Rounded Rectangle tool

The Rounded Rectangle tool helps you create multiple rounded rectangles quickly. Your most recent settings for the corner radii are automatically applied to the initial settings for the Rounded Rectangle tool. Next, you'll create a second rounded rectangle using the Rounded Rectangle tool.

1 Select the Rounded Rectangle tool (R) from the Tools panel above the Properties panel.

2 Click and drag out a rectangle on the Stage.

Notice how the corner radii values are identical to the ones you used for your previous rectangle element.

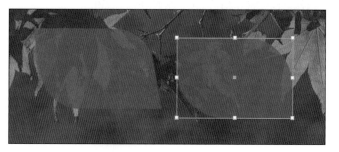

3 Make the W and H properties of your second rounded rectangle identical to the first rounded rectangle, and change the SkewX property to tilt it the same amount.

You now have two identical rounded rectangles on the stage. You could have copied and pasted the elements, or choose Edit > Duplicate to make an exact copy just as well.

Changing the color, opacity, or border

At any time, you can modify the color of your HTML elements. Use the Color section in the Properties panel to change the background color, opacity, or the border color or thickness.

1 Select one of your rounded rectangle elements on the Stage.

2 In the Color section of the Properties panel, click on the background color chip.

The color picker appears.

3 Choose a slightly ruddier color (#a77159) for the second rounded rectangle.

The selected element changes its background color.

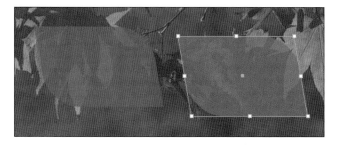

4 Select both of your rounded rectangle elements by holding the Shift key and clicking on each of them.

5 In the Color section of the Properties panel, change the border-style property to Solid and the border-width property from 0 px to 1 px.

A 1-pixel black border appears around both of your rounded rectangle elements, helping distinguish them from the busy background.

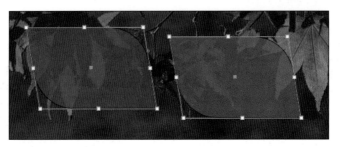

Ellipse tool

For your convenience, Edge Animate also provides an Ellipse tool (O) that works very similarly to the Rectangle and Rounded Rectangle tool. The Ellipse tool creates ellipses and perfect circles (if you hold down the Shift key) by creating a rectangle with its border radii set at 50% by default. Since the border radii is 50% of its width and height, the curvature of its corners will always be rounded enough to create an ellipse or circle.

Working with Rulers and Guides

As you begin to create and arrange more elements on your Stage, it becomes important to be wary of alignments and spacing along a grid. Edge Animate provides several ways to keep your elements laid out in an orderly fashion. You can display rulers on the horizontal and vertical axes. You can also place guides anywhere on the Stage that help align elements, but will not show up in the final composition in the browser. Smart guides automatically appear when you're creating or moving objects so you can quickly move objects to edges or centerpoints of other objects.

The Align and Distribute commands are also indispensable for arranging elements, which you'll learn about later in the lesson.

Using Rulers and Guides

Rulers are static, and measure pixels across and down the Stage, while Guides can be moved around the Stage.

1 Choose View > Rulers or press Ctrl+R (Windows)/Command+R (Mac OS) to enable rulers, if they are not already enabled (a check mark in front of the menu item means that rulers are on).

   Rulers appear on the top and left edge of the Stage, in pixel units.

2 Click on the horizontal Ruler and drag your cursor down to the Stage.

   A Guide appears on the Stage.

3 Move the Guide to about 220 pixels down from the top edge of the Stage.

Note: Unfortunately, you cannot specify a pixel value to place your Guide.

4   Make sure that snapping is enabled (checked) by choosing View > Snap to Guides or pressing Shift+Ctrl+; (Windows)/Shift+Command+; (Mac OS).

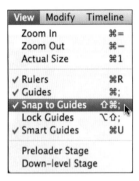

Snap to Guides will force elements on the Stage to snap to the Guides when you move close enough to them.

5   Drag your two rounded rectangle elements so that their top edges snap to the Guide.

Your two rounded rectangle elements are now aligned with the Guide at 220 pixels.

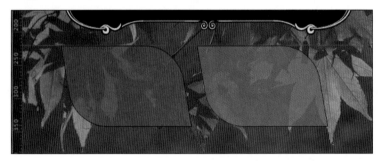

Editing Guides

Guides are easy to work with and to edit.

*   To lock your Guides so you don't accidentally move them, choose View > Lock Guides or press Alt+Shift+; (Windows)/Option+Shift+; (Mac OS).

*   To remove a Guide, simply drag it off the Stage panel.

*   To hide your Guides, choose View > Guides or press Ctrl+; (Windows)/Command+; (Mac OS).

    Edge Animate disables your Guides, and they will no longer be displayed.

Using Smart Guides

Smart Guides are, by default, activated, and provide helpful markers for you to create or move elements relative to other elements on the Stage. Next, you'll create three ellipses that will anchor some text along the bottom of the Stage.

1   Choose the Rectangle tool from the Tools panel, and choose a lemon yellow (#dcd24f) for the background color.

2   Create a small rectangle on the Stage that is 60 pixels wide and 50 pixels tall.

3   In the Corners section of the Properties panel, change the corner radii of all the corners to 60 pixels.

The four corners of your rectangle become rounded, producing an elliptical shape.

4   Press Ctrl+U (Windows)/Command+U (MacOS), if necessary, to make sure that Smart Guides are enabled. The check mark should be in front of the menu item View > Smart Guides.

5   Choose the Rounded Rectangle tool, and keep the background color the same lemon yellow.

6   Begin to drag out a small rounded rectangle.

Edge Animate automatically displays Smart Guides that show you how the dimensions of the element you're creating match up with the other objects on the Stage.

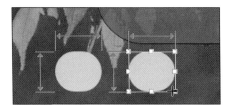

7   Drag out a small ellipsoid shape that is the same width and height as the first one you made.

Matching height and width Smart Guides appear around your rounded rectangles.

8   Create a third rounded rectangle using Smart Guides that is the same height and width as the first two.

Creating text

Every website needs text. Text is not only important for the main body of your site, but for headers, labels, buttons, image captions, and other kinds of descriptive elements.

Edge Animate provides formatting and styling options for text that should be familiar to anyone who has used a word processing or graphics-editing program.

Adding labels

For the next steps in this project, you'll add some text over the rounded rectangles and some text to layer on top of each of the ellipses.

1   Select the Text tool (T) from the Tools panel above the Properties panel.

2   Click on the Stage.

A text-editing window appears on the Stage, and a new text element is created in the Elements and Timeline panel.

3   In the text-editing window, enter **Pastries**.

● **Note:** Pressing the Enter/Return key after you're done creating text will create a new line and won't dismiss the text-editing panel.

4   Click outside the text-editing window, click the Close box in the upper-right corner, or press the Esc key.

The text-editing window disappears, and your text element remains on the Stage at the point of insertion.

Styling the text

You can style the text by choosing a different font face, color, or size, or by varying the letter spacing, line spacing, word spacing, and other layout preferences.

1   While the text element is still selected, choose Georgia, Times New Roman, Times, serif from the Font pulldown menu.

The font choices represent the order of priority for displaying the text. The first choice is Georgia, but if your audience's computer cannot display the text in Georgia, the browser will use the next font in the list. This list is called the font fallback list.

2 Change the font size to 24 pixels.

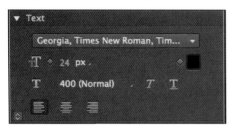

Note: Additional text options are hidden in the Properties panel, accessible when you click on the double-headed arrows in the Text section. The additional options include letter spacing, word spacing, line spacing, and indents.

3 Make sure the font color is black.

Note: The color for your text is represented by the color chip in the Text section of the Properties panel, and not by the color chip in the Tools panel. The color chip in the Text section refers to the color property, while the color chip in the Tools panel refers to the background-color property, which is for your rectangle elements.

Duplicating the text

Like any other element on the Stage, you can copy and paste, or duplicate the elements.

1 Select your newly created text and choose Edit > Duplicate or press Ctrl+D (Windows)/Command+D (Mac OS).

Edge Animate creates a duplicate text element in the same position as the original and selects it by default.

2 Move the duplicated text over to the second yellow ellipse.

3 Duplicate, or copy and paste, the text and move it over to the third yellow ellipse.

You now have three yellow ellipses with the text "Pastries" layered over each of them.

Note: Another quick way to duplicate an element is to hold down the Alt/Option key while you move an element on the Stage. Edge Animate creates an exact copy that you can move to a new position.

UNIVERSITY OF WINCHESTER
LIBRARY

Making text edits

All text elements remain fully editable.

1   Double-click the second text element, or right-click and choose Edit Text from the contextual menu.

The text-editing panel opens, with the current contents of the text selected.

2   Replace the current contents of the text-editing panel by typing **Espresso**.

3   Edit the third text element on the Stage and change the text to **Tea**.

Creating initial fixed-width text

When you click on the Stage to insert a new text element, there is no defined maximum width to the text. As you enter content in the text-editing panel, the text will continue to extend to the right until you press the Enter (Windows)/Return (Mac OS) key to create a new line, or until your text reaches the edge of the Stage.

You can define the initial width of your text box by clicking and dragging a text box with a fixed width on the Stage. You'll create the fixed-width text for the two rounded rectangles.

1   Select the Text tool from the Tools panel above the Properties panel.

2   Click inside the first rounded rectangle and drag out a text box that comfortably fits inside.

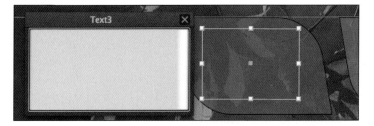

The text-editing panel appears on the Stage.

3 In the text-editing window, enter **Fall has arrived**!

4 Click outside the text-editing window, click the Close box in the upper-right corner, or press the Esc key.

The text-editing window disappears. The fixed width of the text box forces your text to appear on two lines.

Note: New text uses the same settings as the most recently created or edited text, so your new text should be Georgia, 24 pixels, and black.

5 Create a second fixed-width text box over the second rounded rectangle. In the text-editing panel, enter **Enjoy our new maple lattes!**

Note: You can always edit the maximum width of any text element by changing the W value in the Properties panel, or by expanding or contracting the blue bounding box around the selection. Changing the width of text selections forces the contents to reflow to fit.

Embedding custom fonts

Your café advertisement already has all of the text elements, but the text isn't especially expressive. The Georgia font appears rather ordinary and lacks the pizzazz that this client deserves or wants.

You could try to give the text more punch by playing with letter spacing, adding styling such as italics, or by using the Transform tool to add some skew or rotation. But no amount of transformation will elevate the actual typeface. Fortunately, you can embed and add custom fonts, which gives you much more typographic creativity.

Embedding fonts relies on the CSS rule `@font-face`, which tells the browser what font to use and where to find the font description. To use a custom font, you need to provide your font in multiple formats (EOT, SVG, TTF, WOFF) as well as the CSS file that refers to them. A convenient approach is to use a custom font that is already hosted. For example, Google provides a collection of free fonts that you can use. In this exercise, you'll be using Google fonts to embed a custom font for the text in your café advertisement.

Adding a Web font to the Library

Custom fonts, like image assets, are organized in the Library panel. The actual fonts are not stored in your Edge Animate composition. Only the code that references where to find the fonts is saved in the Library panel.

1 In the Fonts section of the Library panel, click the Add Web Font button.

Alternately, when a text element is selected, choose the Add Font option that appears at the bottom of the font pull-down list.

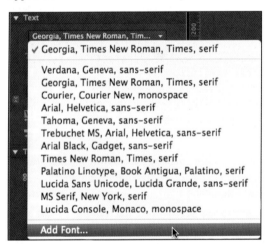

The Add Web Font dialog box appears with two empty fields: Font Fallback List and Embed Code. You'll visit the Google Web Font website to get the required information.

2 In your browser, visit www.google.com/webfonts.

Google displays a huge collection of free custom web fonts, with previews as well as options for filtering the results.

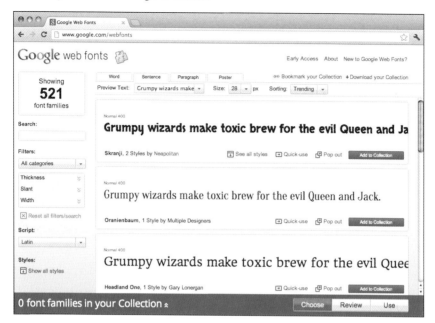

3 Browse the collection for a font that would be appropriate for the café advertisement. In this final project, we've used the Rock Salt font. You can enter **Rock Salt** in the Search box to see the font.

4 Choose the Quick-use link.

Google shows you more information about the selected font, such as the estimated impact on load time and additional options.

5 At the bottom of the page, copy the contents in the Standard field containing the `<link>` tag.

The `<link>` tag contains the URL to the CSS document that points to the required font files.

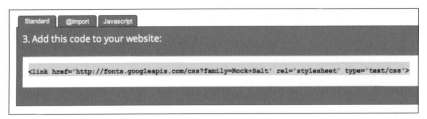

6 Return to Edge Animate, and paste the <link> code in the Embed Code field.

The full code should appear as follows:

```
<link href='http://fonts.googleapis.com/css?family=Rock+Salt'
rel='stylesheet' type='text/css'>
```

7 In the Font Fallback List field, enter '**Rock Salt**'.

Rock Salt is the name of the actual font family.

8 Click on the plus (+) button at the end of the Font Fallback List field, and choose two additional font families, Georgia and sans-serif.

The list of fonts, separated by commas, represents the order of font families that the browser will display for your text, in order of priority.

9 Click Add Font.

Edge Animate saves the font information in the Library panel.

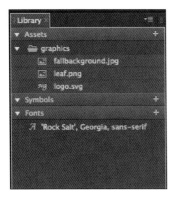

Applying a web font

Custom fonts that are added to the Library panel are also added to the font pull-down list in the Properties panel so you can apply them to your text elements.

1   Select all the text elements on your Stage. The three labels on the ellipses and the two descriptions in the rounded rectangles should be all selected.

2   In the Properties panel, choose 'Rock Salt', Georgia, sans-serif from the fonts pull-down menu.

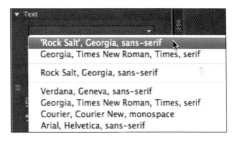

● **Note:** You'll need an Internet connection to see the custom fonts when you preview your composition. Your custom fonts depend on downloading the font information from Google, where they are hosted.

Your text displays with the custom web font from Google.

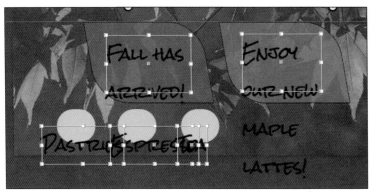

● **Note:** Limit the number of web fonts in your Edge Animate compositions. Each new font family adds another download burden to your site.

Refining the text

The new Rock Salt font changes the way your text is laid out on the Stage, so a little refinement is necessary. Use the additional (and hidden) formatting options in the Text section of the Properties panel to tighten the line spacing and font sizes, where necessary.

1 Select the text inside the first rounded rectangle, "Fall has arrived!", and click the double-headed arrow to access the additional text-formatting properties in the Properties panel. Change the line-height value to 35 pixels.

2 Select the text inside the second rounded rectangle, "Try our new maple lattes!", and change the line-height value to 30 pixels and the font size to 21 pixels.

The new Rock Salt font fits comfortably within the rectangle elements.

The alphabet soup of web font formats

Web fonts are complicated because different browsers support different font formats. At the time of this publication, Internet Explorer supports only the EOT (Embedded Open Type) format. Mozilla browsers support OTF and TTF (Open Type Font and True Type Font) formats. Safari and Opera browsers support OTF, TTF, and SVG (Scalable Vector Graphics) file types. Google Chrome supports TTF and SVG. Mobile browsers such as Safari on the iPad and iPhone require SVG. In order to make your content viewable to the widest audience, you must convert your fonts to all formats and make them available, which makes hosted fonts like Google Fonts particularly convenient and attractive.

Tidying up your elements

Your composition currently consists of multiple elements—bitmaps, SVG graphics, and HTML rectangles, and text. Earlier you learned how to use the Rulers and Guides to keep elements aligned, but when dealing with aligning multiple objects to each other, it's best to use the Align commands.

Aligning elements

The Modify > Align command moves all the selected objects on the Stage in alignment with their left, right, top, or bottom edges, or centerlines. You'll use the Align option to center the text over their rounded rectangles.

1   Select the first rounded rectangle and the text that is over it ("Fall has arrived!").

2   Choose Modify > Align > Horizontal Center, and then choose Modify > Align > Vertical Center.

The two selected elements move so that both their vertical and horizontal centerlines match, resulting in text that is perfectly centered over the rounded rectangular element. Edge Animate uses the bounding box for both elements to make the alignments.

3   Select the second rounded rectangle and the text that is over it ("Enjoy our new maple lattes!").

4   Choose Modify > Align > Horizontal Center, and then choose Modify > Align > Vertical Center.

The text becomes centered over the rounded rectangular element.

5　Repeat the process of aligning along the horizontal and vertical centers for each of the text elements and the ellipsoid shapes below them.

Organizing your elements

The next step for your composition is to distribute the text elements and their rounded rectangles evenly on the Stage. The three elements—Pastries, Espresso, and Tea—should have consistent spacing between them, as should the two text elements above them.

You can use the Distribute command, but you need to keep the text and the rectangle below them together as a single unit. In Edge Animate, as in other graphics-editing programs, you can group elements together. Grouped elements become part of a larger div element that can be animated, moved, or transformed just like any other element on the Stage.

Grouping elements

You can group two or more elements together with the Group Elements in DIV feature.

1　Select the first text element and the rounded rectangle below it.

2　Choose Modify > Group Elements in DIV or press Ctrl+G (Windows) or Command+G (Mac OS).

The two selected elements are put inside a div element. The hierarchy is reflected in the Elements panel, where the two elements appear below the group name.

3 Rename the group **tagline1group**.

4 Select and group all the other text and their respective box elements.

5 Rename the groups **tagline2group**, **pastriesgroup**, **espressogroup**, and **teagroup**.

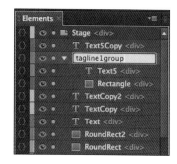

Note: Clicking on any element in a group on the Stage will automatically select the entire group. Use the Elements panel to select individual elements of a group.

Note: Effects, such as transformations or opacity changes, can be applied to the individual elements in a group, or to the entire group.

Distributing elements

Now that taglines and other text elements are grouped with their underlying graphics, you can distribute them across the Stage evenly.

1 Select the pastriesgroup element, and move it so its left edge aligns with the left edge of the SVG logo. You can use the Smart Guides to make the alignment.

2 Select the teagroup element, and move it so its right edge aligns with the right edge of the SVG logo. You can use the Smart Guides to make the alignment.

3 Select the pastriesgroup, espressogroup, and teagroup elements.

4 Choose Modify > Distribute > Left.

Edge Animate distributes the spacing of the elements between the far-left and far-right elements so that their *left* edges are equally spaced apart. Your three groups are now evenly distributed.

● **Note:** You can't use the Distribute command on your tagline1group and tagline2group elements because the Distribute command works only for groups with three or more elements.

5 Choose Modify > Align > Bottom.

Edge Animate aligns the bottom edges of all three groups.

Modifying and editing groups

Additional elements can easily be added to existing groups, and the individual elements within a group can be edited or deleted.

- **To delete a group**, select the group, and press the Delete key.

- **To add an element to a group**, drag a new element and drop it onto the group in the Elements panel.

  The new element becomes part of the group, and the Elements panel displays it as another indented item under the group.

- **To remove an element from a group**, drag the element from its indented position under the group in a new position in the Elements panel outside the group.

- **To delete an element in a group**, select the element in the Elements or Timeline panel and press the Delete key.

  Edge Animate removes the selected element from the group.

- **To ungroup the elements of a group**, select the group and choose Modify > Ungroup Elements or press Shift+Ctrl+G (Windows)/Shift+Command+G (Mac OS).

Understanding element hierarchies

When you group elements, Edge Animate essentially creates an element hierarchy with an empty div as the parent element. The empty div is the container in which all your grouped elements live.

You can create other element hierarchies by simply dragging an element on top of another element in the Elements panel. You create a parent-child hierarchy with your two elements. Only elements created from the Rectangle tool can be the parent element, and only rectangles, text, or images can be its children. Any transformation or any effects applied to the parent will also affect the children.

Adding special effects

A drop shadow can have a dramatic effect on your composition, and help separate the foreground elements from the background. Edge Animate provides many options to apply shadows to your elements, including the direction, amount of blur, color, opacity, and whether your shadow is an inset shadow or a drop shadow.

Applying drop shadows

You'll add a drop shadow to each of the rounded rectangles in the tagline1group and the tagline2group elements. The shadows will provide some focus to those particular graphics.

1   In the Elements panel, select the rounded rectangle in the tagline1group element.

● Note: Use the Toggle option for the Shadow in the Properties panel to quickly turn the effect on or off. When turned on, the Shadow settings are summarized at the head of the section for your convenience.

2   Expand the Shadow section of the Properties panel, and toggle the Shadow effect on.

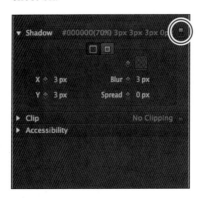

3   Choose black (#000000) for the color and an Alpha (A) value of 70%.

4   Enter these values for the shadow: X=10 pixels, Y=10 pixels, Blur=5 pixels, and Spread=0 pixels.

The drop shadow appears 10 pixels to the right and 10 pixels from the bottom of the rectangle, with a 5-pixel blur, and no spread, which means that the shadow is the same size as the rectangle.

5   Select the rounded rectangle in the tagline2group element in the Elements panel and enter the same values for its drop shadow in the Properties panel.

Making rotations

You've already used the Transformation tool earlier in this lesson to skew your rounded rectangles. You can also use the Transformation tool or the Properties panel to rotate your elements. Rotations are always made around an origin point, which by default, is at the center of your object. However, you have the option to move the origin point for more precise control over your rotations.

Rotate elements

In this exercise, you'll rotate the tagline1group and tagline2group elements to break up the formality of the layout.

1 Select the tagline1group element on the Stage.

2 Select the Transform tool from the Tools panel above the Properties panel.

    A dark bounding box with black control points appears around the selected element.

3 Move your cursor close to one of the corner points of the bounding box until your cursor changes to a rotate icon.

Note: It's important that you select the entire group before making the rotation. If you select just the text or the box under it, you'll only rotate those elements within the group.

4 Click and drag the transform bounding box on the Stage.

    The selected element rotates freely. You can also see the changing values for the Rotate property in the Transform section of the Properties panel. Change the rotation value to −11 degrees.

5 Select the tagline2group element on the Stage.

    A dark bounding box with black control points appears around the selected element.

6 Move your cursor close to one of the corner points of the bounding box until your cursor changes to a rotate icon.

Note: You can change the value of an element's rotation entirely with the Properties panel as easily as you can with the Transformation tool.

7   Click and drag the transform bounding box on the Stage.

The selected element rotates freely. Change the rotation value to 7 degrees.

Changing the center of rotation

The rotation of the tagline1group and tagline2group elements revolves around their centerpoints. However, you may need or want to rotate an element around a different point.

For example, let's say that your client wants you to rotate the PNG image of the leaf in the top corner. In order to do so, it would be convenient to keep its point of rotation the same as the point of attachment at the base of the stem. In order to do that, you need to change its registration point. Rotating the leaf around the base of its stem will make animating it much more realistic.

1   Select the leaf element on the Stage, Timeline, or Elements panel.

2   Move the leaf element to the top of the Elements stack so it overlaps all the other elements on the Stage.

3   Select the Transform tool from the Tools panel above the Properties panel.

A dark bounding box with black control points appears around the selected element. The crosshair icon in the center of the bounding box represents the origin of transformation, which is the point around which all transformations are performed.

4 Click and drag the origin of transformation near the top edge of the bounding box.

Origin of transformation

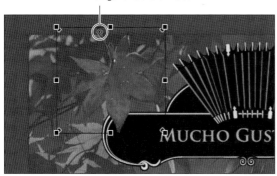

The resulting Origin properties in the Transform section of the Properties panel should be X=40% and Y=5%.

5 Rotate the selected leaf element so the Rotate property is 22 degrees.

The leaf element rotates around the new registration point at the base of its stem.

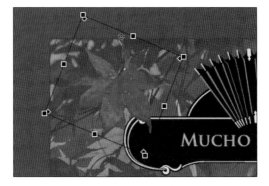

Note: The origin of transformation of an element can be outside of its bounding box, which means that the element would revolve around an outside axis. For example, a circle with its origin point outside of its bounding box would rotate like a planet revolving around the sun.

Taking a closer look

If you're having trouble moving the registration point of the leaf element to the exact spot at the base of its stem, you may need to zoom in closer. From the top menu, choose View > Zoom In or press Ctrl+= (Windows)/Command+= (Mac OS) to zoom into the Stage for more precise positioning. Scroll bars around the Stage appear so you can move around the zoomed-up Stage.

To zoom out, choose View > Zoom Out or press Ctrl+- (Windows)/Command+- (Mac OS), and to return to actual size, choose View > Actual Size or press Ctrl+1 (Windows)/Command+1 (Mac OS).

Animating a rotation

As the final touch for this composition, you'll add a leisurely rotation to the leaf to have it rock back and forth in a slight breeze.

1 Select the leaf element.

2 Make sure that your playhead on the Timeline is at 0:00 and the Auto-Keyframe and the Auto-Transition modes are enabled.

3 In the Timeline panel, select the leaf element and right-click and choose Add Keyframe > Rotate (z).

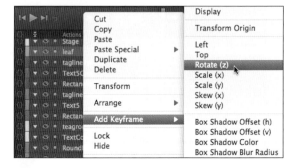

Alternately, click on the Add Keyframe for Rotate icon in the Properties panel.

A keyframe for the Rotate property appears in the Timeline.

4 Move your playhead out to 1:00 second.

5 Select the Transform tool from the Tools panel above the Properties panel.

A dark bounding box appears around the selected element.

6 Rotate the leaf so that the Rotate property is about 2 degrees.

A new keyframe for the Rotate property appears in the Timeline at 1:00 second, and Edge Animate creates a smooth animation between 0:00 and 1:00 seconds.

7 Continue moving the playhead along the Timeline and rotating the leaf so it sways back and forth slowly. You may need several keyframes spaced several seconds apart. Be creative!

Review questions

1   How does an SVG graphic differ from a JPEG file?

2   Where are imported images stored?

3   What is a group and how is it useful?

4   What kind of effects can the Transform tool make on an element?

5   How do you apply a web font to a text element?

Review answers

1   A Scalable Vector Graphic, or SVG file, is a vector-based image file. SVG images are resolution-independent, which means that they can be scaled without losing any image quality. JPEG files, on the other hand, are bitmaps, which means that their image is described by fixed pixels.

2   Images imported into Edge Animate are not stored in the composition. Rather, the path to the file is saved in the Library panel. The default folder where Edge Animate looks for image assets is in a folder called images, but image assets can be organized in any folder or subfolder of the same directory as the Edge Animate source file.

3   A group is a collection of elements that are organized as children of a parent div element. Transformations and animations on the parent element affect all the elements in the group. Use groups to keep many similar elements as a single unit for editing, aligning, and distributing, and for animation.

4   The Transform tool can resize, skew, and rotate elements, and change the border radii of rectangular elements.

5   Add a web font by clicking the Add Web Font button next to the Font section of the Library panel. In the Add Web Font dialog box, list the fonts in the Font Fallback List, and enter the <link> tag that contains the URL to the CSS document that points to the required font files.

3 DESIGNING ANIMATION

Lesson Overview

In this lesson, you'll learn how to do the following:

- Animate various properties of elements
- Use the Pin and the playhead
- Animate with Auto-Keyframe and Auto-Transition modes
- Edit keyframes to change pacing and timing
- Lengthen or shorten an animation
- Create fade-in and fade-out transitions by animating opacity
- Copy and paste animation
- Reverse an animation
- Create abrupt visual changes
- Use placeholder assets and swap assets
- Apply easing curves to an animation
- Add a web font

 This lesson will take about two hours to complete. Open the Lesson03 folder from the *Adobe Edge Animate Classroom in a Book* lesson files to begin.

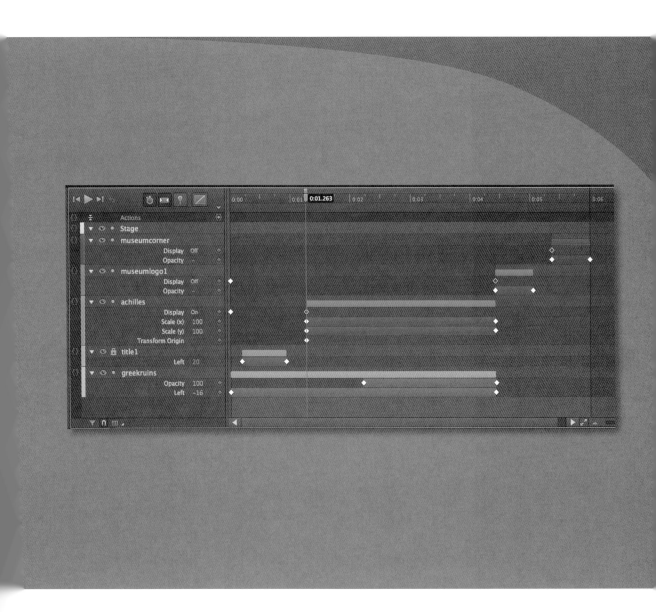

Make visually compelling motion graphics with Edge Animate's intuitive and powerful interface. You control the timing and pacing of the change of properties for all your visual elements.

Getting started

In this lesson, you'll learn the different ways you can add motion and transitions to create an effective and attractive animated ad.

1 Choose File > Open or click the Open File link from the Getting Started opening panel. In the Open dialog box, select the 03End.an file in the Lesson03/03End folder and click Open to see the final project.

2 Choose File > Preview in Browser, or press Ctrl+Enter (Windows)/ Cmd+Return (Mac OS).

Edge Animate creates the necessary files to display the final animation in your default browser, which opens automatically. The browser shows an animated ad for a fictional museum exhibit. An image of an ancient Greek temple pans across the screen as some text moves across it in the opposite direction. A vignetted image of the Greek hero Achilles pops into view, superimposed on the background image. The ad ends when additional informational text slowly fades in.

3 Close the browser.

4 In Edge Animate, choose File > New or Ctrl+N (Windows)/Command+N (Mac OS) to start a new document.

5 In the Properties panel, change the Stage size to 240 pixels wide and 400 pixels high, which is one of the standard sizes for a rectangular banner ad. Choose black (#000000) for the background color of the Stage.

6 In the composition title field at the top of the Properties panel, name your Edge Animate composition **Museum of Greek Antiquities**.

7 Save your file as **03_workingcopy** in the 03Start folder.

About animation

Animation is simply the change of one or more of an element's properties through time. If an element's position changes through time, we know it as motion. Many other properties can change. For example, an element's opacity can change over time. If an object begins with 0% opacity and, at a later time, ends with 100% opacity, we see the element fade in.

In this lesson, you'll learn to animate many different aspects of a single element in Edge Animate. You can even animate multiple properties of a single element at the same time. You can change an element's position on the Stage, change its color or opacity, its size or its rotation, and even animate the drop shadows you worked with in the previous lesson. You also have control over the easing, which is the rate of change at which an animation proceeds.

The essence of animation lies in understanding keyframes. A keyframe in Edge Animate appears as a diamond on the Timeline panel. A keyframe indicates the point in time when there is a change in an element's property. An animation requires that you define at least two keyframes—a beginning keyframe that establishes the initial value of a property, and the end keyframe that establishes the final value. To create an animation, Edge Animate interpolates the smooth changes in the property between the two keyframes. The animation between two keyframes appears as a colored bar on the Timeline panel.

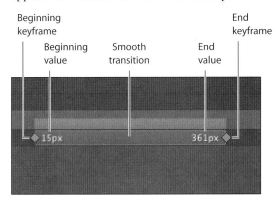

Keyframing is a common concept among animators and harkens back to the days of classic hand-drawn animation. Senior animators would be responsible for drawing the beginning and ending poses for their characters, which are the most important for defining the motion. The beginning and end poses were the keyframes of the animation. Junior animators would then come in and draw the in-between frames. So you can think of yourself as the senior animator, and Edge Animate as your loyal assistant!

Understanding the project file

All the visual elements, except for some text, are provided for you to build the fictional animated banner ad. In this lesson, your efforts are focused on animating the elements rather than creating them. Examine the 03Start folder and open the images folder inside of it. The images of the Greek temple, Achilles, two versions of the museum logo, and a corner graphic are sized correctly and ready for your Edge Animate composition.

Turn your attention to your new Edge Animate composition, 03_workingcopy. In the Library, notice that the image assets are already listed within the images folder.

Edge Animate automatically assumes that you will organize your images within a folder called "images," so Edge Animate compositions that are saved in the same directory as an images folder will display the folder's contents in the Library for your convenience. You can always organize your assets differently and use the Import command (File > Import, Ctrl/Command+I) to establish the relative path from the image to your Edge Animate file. However, the path must point to a folder within the same directory or in a subdirectory of your Edge Animate file.

Animating position with the Pin

You'll build the animated banner ad from the bottom up, meaning you'll start with the bottom-most image and gradually add the overlapping elements.

You'll use the Pin to create motion. The Pin is a unique Edge Animate tool that allows you to create both the beginning and ending keyframes with a single edit.

Importing the background image

The first image you'll work with is the Greek temple. The image begins on the right side of the Stage, and then slowly moves to the left side of the Stage, making it appear as though the camera is panning across the ruins.

1   Expand the images folder within the Assets section of your Library panel.

   The image files in the images folder appear.

2 Drag the greekruins.jpg file from the Library onto the Stage. Position the top-left corner of the image at the top-left corner of the Stage. The coordinates near your cursor should read (0,0).

Edge Animate displays the X- and Y-coordinates of the image file as you move it over the Stage. Edge Animate also displays smart guides to help you position the image flush against the top and left edges of the Stage.

The element called greekruins appears in both the Elements and Timeline panels.

Using the Pin to create keyframes

In order to make the image of the Greek temple move from the right to the left, you'll create an initial keyframe at its current position, and then create a final keyframe where the temple is at a different position. The Pin, represented by the blue teardrop-shaped marker when active, helps you make those keyframes all at once.

The Pin works by "pinning" or fixing the current values of your element. You can then move the playhead to a different position on the Timeline and change the properties of your element. Edge Animate will create the keyframes to animate *from* the Pin *to* the playhead.

Note: If Auto-Keyframe or Auto-Transition mode is off, then Edge Animate turns both modes on when you activate the Pin. The Pin only works in conjunction with Auto-Keyframe and Auto-Transition modes enabled.

1   Activate the Pin by clicking on the Pin icon, or double-click the playhead. You can also toggle the Pin by pressing the P key on the keyboard.

The Pin turns blue, indicating that it is activated.

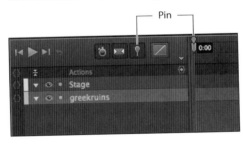

2   Drag the playhead on the Timeline to 0:02 seconds.

The playhead and the Pin separate. The Pin remains at 0:00 seconds, and a gold-colored band of arrows appears between the Pin and the playhead. The direction of the arrows represents the direction of the animation. Since the current position of the image is at the location of the Pin, any changes to the image at the current playhead will result in an animation that proceeds from a keyframe at the Pin to a new keyframe at the playhead.

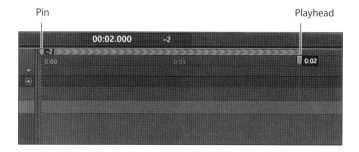

Pin   Playhead

Note: Make sure that you drag the playhead, and not the Pin, out to 0:02 seconds.

It's a little confusing at first, but with patience and practice, you'll get more comfortable with the basic workflow.

3 Move the image of the Greek temple to the left so its right edge aligns with the right edge of the Stage. The X-property of the image should be at –57 pixels.

Edge Animate automatically inserts a new keyframe at 0:02 seconds. A new lane for the Left property appears under the greekruins element in the Timeline to show its change in the horizontal position from 0:00 seconds to 0:002 seconds.

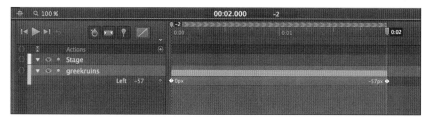

4 Click on the Pin to turn it off.

5 Press the spacebar.

Edge Animate previews the animation. The playhead moves from the start of the Timeline to the end of the animation, showing the image moving on the Stage. The timecode just below the Stage displays the number of seconds elapsed as the animation plays.

Adding the moving title

Now you'll add a second moving element. The title will move quickly onto the Stage from the opposite direction. You'll use the Pin and the playhead to create the beginning and ending keyframes for the animation in one edit.

1 Make sure that your current playhead is at the end of the animation, at 0:02 seconds.

2 Select the Text tool and drag out a text box on the left side of the Stage about half the width of the Stage.

A text-editing box appears next to the text field.

3 Enter the title, **Discover an Ancient World**, in the text editor.

4 In the Properties panel, choose Arial for the font family, 24 pixels for the font size, and white (#ffffff) for the font color.

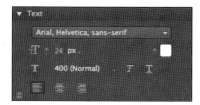

The new text element appears in your Timeline and Elements panel. Rename the text element **title1**.

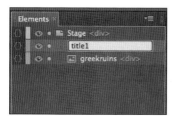

You'll edit the style of the text to sharpen its appearance in the next section of this lesson.

5 In the Properties panel, move the text so X=20 and Y=20.

These coordinates represent the ending position of the title.

6 Activate the Pin by clicking on the Pin icon, or double-click the playhead. You can also toggle the Pin by pressing the P key on the keyboard.

The Pin turns blue, indicating that it is activated.

7 Drag the playhead on the Timeline back to 0:00 seconds.

The playhead and the Pin separate. The Pin remains at 0:02 seconds, and a blue-colored band of arrows appears between the Pin and the playhead. The arrows point backward because the playhead is behind the Pin, which is a reminder that you'll be creating the beginning keyframe *after* the ending keyframe is already set.

8 While holding down the Shift key, move the title off the Stage to the left. The coordinates of the title should be X=−130, Y=20.

Edge Animate creates the beginning keyframe at 0:00 seconds when the title is off the Stage and an ending keyframe at 0:02 seconds when the title is on the Stage.

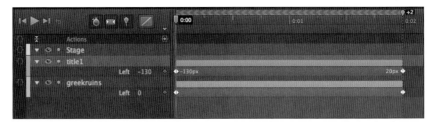

9 Click on the Pin to turn it off.

10 Press the spacebar.

Edge Animate previews the animation. The playhead moves from the start of the Timeline to the end of the animation, showing the image moving from right to left at the same time the text moves in the opposite direction.

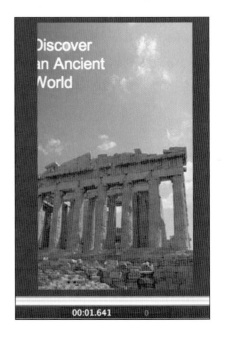

Adding a web font

In the previous lesson, you learned to embed a Web font from Google Fonts for custom type treatment. Here, you'll add a Web font that is suggestive of classical Greece to spruce up the title.

1   In the Library, click the Add Web Font button (the plus sign) next to the Fonts section.

The Add Web Font dialog box appears.

2   In the Font Fallback List field, enter the following:

`'IM Fell French Canon SC', 'Times', 'serif'`

The Font Fallback List provides a list of fonts to use, in order of preference, in case the desired font is unavailable on the user's machine. Our choice of font is a Google font called IM Fell French Canon SC.

3   In the Embed Code field, enter the following:

`<link href='http://fonts.googleapis.com/css?family=IM+Fell+French+Canon+SC' rel='stylesheet' type='text/css'>`

The Embed Code provides the path to the Google font.

4   Click Add font.

Edge Animate saves the font information in the Library panel.

5   Select the title element on the Stage, Timeline, or Elements panel.

6 In the Property panel, choose the IM Fell French Canon SC option in the font family pull-down menu.

Your title uses the selected font for a more elegant presentation.

Changing pacing and timing

You can change the duration of the entire animation or change the timing of the animation by clicking and dragging keyframes on the Timeline.

Changing the animation duration

If you want the animation to proceed at a slower pace, taking up a much longer period of time, you need to lengthen the entire span between the beginning and end keyframes. If you want to shorten the animation, you need to decrease the span. Lengthen or shorten an animation by dragging the keyframes closer or farther apart on the Timeline.

1 Move your mouse cursor over the end keyframe at the end of the animation span for the title1 element.

Your cursor changes to a double-headed arrow, indicating that you can move the keyframe.

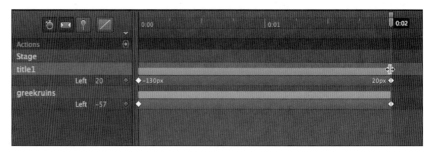

2 Click and drag the keyframe back to 0:00.500 seconds.

Your animation shortens to half a second.

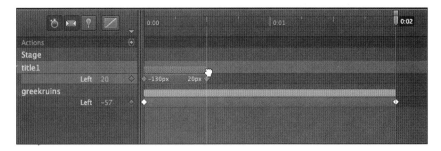

3 Press the spacebar to play the animation.

The animation for title1 has a much shorter time to move, so it moves quickly.

Adding time

Currently, your Edge Animate composition lasts for a total of 2 seconds, which may be a little too short for your audience to appreciate the animation. You can easily lengthen your animation by dragging the ending keyframes farther from their beginning keyframes. However, an easier approach for adding time to the entire Timeline is to choose Timeline > Insert Time from the top menu.

1 Move the playhead to 0:00.250 seconds.

The playhead is positioned at a point in time that is between the keyframes of both of your moving elements.

2 From the top menu, choose Timeline > Insert Time.

The Insert Time dialog box appears.

3 Enter **00:00.500** in the Amount of time to insert field.

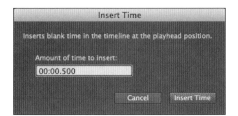

4 Click Insert Time.

Edge Animate adds the specified amount of time at the position of the playhead. The animation of the title and the animation of the Greek temple each become a half a second longer.

Note: Be aware of the position of your playhead when you insert time with Timeline > Insert Time. If you were to place your playhead between the keyframes of the Greek temple motion and not the title motion, then only the animation of the Greek temple would lengthen.

Note: Unfortunately, there is no opposite to the Insert Time command that would remove time from the top menu. To remove time, simply click and drag the end keyframes of your animation to shorten each animation. You can also select multiple elements and then click and drag the end of the animation span to shorten all the selected elements proportionally.

Changing the timing of an animation

In Edge Animate, you can move not only individual keyframes, but the entire animation span forward or backward in time as a single unit. This allows you to control the timing of the animation in relation to other animated elements.

1 Move your cursor over the animation span for the title1 element in the Timeline panel.

   Your cursor turns to a hand icon, indicating that you can move the animation span.

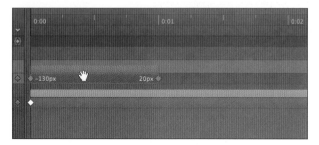

2 Click and drag the span forward on the Timeline so it begins at 0:00.250 seconds.

3 Press the spacebar to play the animation.

   The animation for title1 now begins a split second after the image begins to move.

Turning the display on and off

Next, you'll add the image of Achilles. The image appears suddenly after the animation of the title and the Greek temple finishes. You can control when an element appears or disappears suddenly from the Stage with the Display property. The Display property is either on, which means the element is visible, or it is off, which means the element is invisible.

Hiding Achilles

Next, you'll add an initial keyframe for the image of Achilles, and set the value for its Display property to Off to hide the element.

1 Drag the image file achilles.png from the Library panel to the Stage.

The image is larger than the Stage and has a transparent background. The element called achilles is added to the Elements and Timeline panels.

2 In the Property panel, position the image at X=−190 and Y=−423.

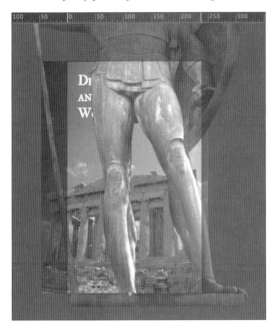

3 Press the spacebar to play the animation.

The animation of the Greek temple and the title proceeds while the static image of Achilles remains on the top layer.

4 Drag the playhead back to 0:00 seconds.

UNIVERSITY OF WINCHESTER
LIBRARY

5 In the Property panel, click the Add Keyframe diamond for the Display property.

Edge Animate inserts a new keyframe for the Display property at 0:00 seconds.

6 In the Property panel, choose Off from the pulldown menu for the Display property value. Or, in the Timeline panel, click the Display property value to toggle it to Off.

The Display property for the achilles element turns off, and Edge Animate hides the image from view. A gray-striped pattern appears over the lane for the achilles element in the Timeline panel, which indicates that the element is invisible.

Making Achilles appear

Achilles should make his appearance at the end of the current animation, so you'll insert a new keyframe at 0:02 seconds and turn the Display property to On.

1 Drag the playhead to 0:02 seconds.

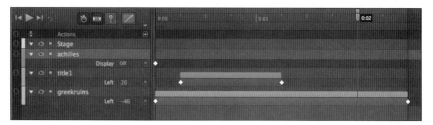

2 In the Timeline panel, make sure that Auto-Keyframe mode is on.

Auto-Keyframe mode is on when the red timer icon is displayed. When Auto-Keyframe mode is on, Edge Animate automatically adds the appropriate keyframes when you make changes to elements.

3 Select the achilles element in the Timeline or in the Elements panel.

Since the element is invisible, you must select it in the Timeline or Elements panel before changing its Display property.

4 In the Properties panel, choose On for the Display property. Or, in the Timeline panel, click the Display property value to toggle it to On.

Edge Animate automatically inserts a new keyframe for the Display property at 0:02 seconds, and sets the value to On.

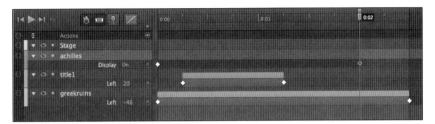

5 Press the spacebar to play the animation.

The animation of the Greek temple and the title proceeds, and the image of Achilles suddenly appears near the end at 0:02 seconds.

Animating scale

So far in this lesson, you've animated the positions of your elements, creating motion for the Greek temple image and the title that runs across it. Next, you'll explore animation of another property: scale.

Changing the scale of an element

In the finished banner ad, the image of Achilles makes a dramatic appearance on the Stage at such a large size that we only see a portion of his legs. Then, the statue gradually becomes smaller to eventually reveal its entirety. The slow animation helps build anticipation and keep the audience interested in the ad.

You can animate the statue getting smaller by changing the values of its Transform properties. The scale of an element is the percentage of its original size. The scale is controlled by the Transform properties for the horizontal dimension (scaleX) and the vertical dimension (scaleY).

1 Move the playhead to 0:02 seconds.

2 In the Timeline panel, turn on the Pin.

Note: Use the Zoom Timeline controls at the bottom right of the Timeline to zoom out to see everything on your Timeline.

3 Drag the playhead to the 0:07 second mark on the Timeline.

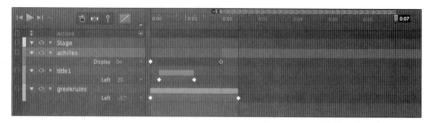

The playhead and the Pin separate. The Pin remains at 0:02 seconds, and a gold-colored band of arrows appears between the Pin and the playhead.

4 Select the achilles element on the Stage, Timeline, or Elements panel.

5 *Do one of the following:*

- In the Properties panel, click and drag over the scaleX Transform value to change it to 50%. Make sure that the Link Scale icon is intact so the horizontal and vertical dimensions remain proportional.

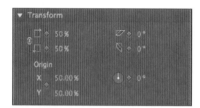

- Select the Transform tool in the Tools panel and drag the corner points of the bounding box inward to shrink the element. Hold down the Shift key to constrain the horizontal and vertical dimensions.

Edge Animate automatically inserts a beginning and ending keyframe for two properties on the Timeline: one for Scale (x) and another for Scale (y). A colored band appears between the beginning and ending keyframes, indicating a smooth animation for the change in scale.

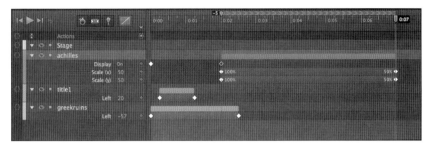

6   Turn the Pin off and press the spacebar on your keyboard to play the animation.

After the initial animation of the Greek temple and title, the image of Achilles appears suddenly and then gradually shrinks. However, the effect isn't satisfactory. The statue changes scale around its default transformation point, which is at the center of the image, so the final image ends up floating in the middle of the Stage.

In the next section, you'll change the origin of transformation so you can precisely control the point around which your element shrinks.

Note: You can also animate an element getting bigger or smaller by changing its W or H properties in the Position and Size section of the Properties panel. The W and H properties control an element's width and height. However, if you use the W and H properties to animate the appearance of an element, the element grows or shrinks relative to its default reference point at the upper-left corner, and you cannot change the origin of transformation like you can with the scaleX or scaleY property.

Changing the origin of transformation

By default, the origin of transformation of any element is located at its center. The *origin* is the point around which rotation, skew, and scale transformations are performed. In this section, you'll move the origin of transformation so the statue of Achilles shrinks around its base, keeping the image on the Stage.

1   Select the Scale (x) and Scale (y) properties on the Timeline and press the Delete key.

The animation to scale the image is deleted so you can start again from scratch.

2   Move the playhead to 0:02 seconds.

3   Make sure that Auto-Keyframe mode is on.

4 Select the Transform tool and click on the statue of Achilles on the Stage.

A black bounding box with control points appears around the image. The origin of transformation is indicated by a crosshairs icon in the middle of the image.

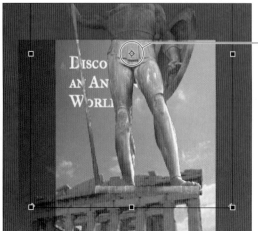

Origin of transformation

5 Drag the origin of transformation to the bottom of the image, at the base of the statue's pedestal. In the Properties panel, the Origin values should be X=50% and Y=93%.

Edge Animate automatically creates a keyframe for the Origin properties for the achilles element in the Timeline panel.

Any subsequent transformations on the achilles element will be done relative to the lower origin of transformation.

6 As in the previous section, turn on the Pin.

7 Drag the playhead to the 0:07 second mark on the Timeline.

The playhead and the Pin separate. The Pin remains at 0:02 seconds, and a gold-colored band of arrows appears between the Pin and the playhead.

8 Select the achilles element on the Stage, Timeline, or Elements panel.

9 In the Properties panel, click and drag over the scaleX value to change it to 50%. Make sure that the Link Scale icon is intact so the horizontal and vertical dimensions remain proportional.

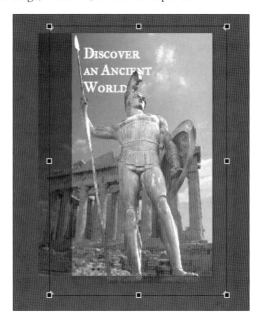

Edge Animate automatically inserts a beginning and ending keyframe for two properties on the Timeline: one for Scale (x) and another for Scale (y). A colored band appears between the beginning and ending keyframes, indicating a smooth animation for the change in scale.

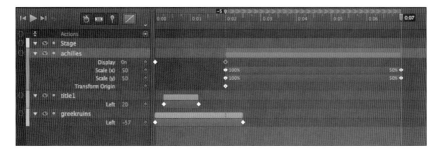

10 Turn the Pin off and press the spacebar to play the animation.

After the initial animation of the Greek temple and title, the image of Achilles appears suddenly, and then gradually shrinks. This time, however, the statue shrinks around its pedestal, keeping its feet firmly planted on the Stage.

Auto-Keyframe and Auto-Transition modes

So far, you've been working with Auto-Keyframe and Auto-Transition modes enabled, so Edge Animate automatically inserts keyframes whenever you make property changes, and automatically inserts smooth transtitions between those keyframes. However, in some situations, you may not want smooth transitions between your keyframes. Disabling Auto-Transition mode lets you create immediate, or abrupt, changes between keyframes without transitions.

For example, you may want a staccato effect to attract more attention where an element appears in different locations. If you move an element around the Stage with Auto-Keyframe mode on and Auto-Transition mode off, your element will change locations without any smooth transitions in between keyframes.

In this Timeline, the Top and Left properties change for the object element in each of its five keyframes, without any transitions.

Creating fades

A fade is when an element slowly disappears or appears on the Stage. A fade helps as a transition between two scenes or as a smooth and gradual introduction or elimination of an element.

You create a fade effect by changing the opacity of an element. When an element's opacity changes from 0% to 100%, it fades into view, and when its opacity changes from 100% to 0%, it fades out of view. You can also change the opacity of an element so it doesn't completely disappear, but remains semitransparent. Use semitransparencies to have elements recede from view and to prevent them from competing with other, more important elements.

Animating a change in opacity

To help keep the focus on the statue of Achilles when it appears, you'll create a slight change of opacity in the Greek temple background so it fades slightly from view.

1   Move the playhead to the point when the title stops moving.

You'll begin the fade-out effect of the Greek temple background at this point.

2   In the Timeline, turn on the Pin.

3   Drag the playhead to the 0:02.500 second mark on the Timeline, just when the Greek temple background stops moving.

The playhead and the Pin separate. A gold-colored band of arrows appears between the Pin and the playhead.

4   Select the greekruins element on the Timeline or Elements panel.

Since the statue of Achilles is on top of the other elements on the Stage, it's easiest to select the Greek ruins image from the Timeline or the Elements panel.

5   In the Properties panel, change the Opacity property to 60%.

Edge Animate automatically inserts a beginning and ending kefyrame for the Opacity property on the Timeline. A colored band appears between the beginning and ending keyframes, indicating a smooth partial fade-out effect of the Greek ruins image from 100% to 60% opacity.

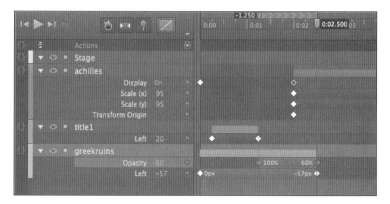

6 Turn the Pin off and press the spacebar to play the animation.

The greekruins element performs two animations: a change in position, and a little while later, a change in opacity.

Animating a fade-in effect

The next graphic to appear in the banner ad is the information about the location and the duration of this fictional exhibit. The information is contained in the PNG image called museumlogo1.png, which is in the images folder.

You'll add the graphic to appear at the end of the animation, but rather than appearing suddenly, you'll create a fade-in effect by animating its opacity values.

1 Select the achilles element on the Stage, Elements, or Timeline panel.

2 Drag the image, museumlogo1.png, from the Library panel to the Stage.

The museumlogo1.png file appears on the Stage above the selected item (the statue of Achilles).

3 Position the museumlogo1 element at X=5 and Y=265.

4 Move the playhead to 0:00 seconds.

5 While the museumlogo1 element is still selected, choose Off from the pull-down menu for Display in the Property panel.

Edge Animate hides the museumlogo1 element at 0:00 seconds.

6 Move the playhead to the end of the composition timeline, at 0:07 seconds.

7 Choose On from the pull-down menu for Display in the Property panel, or click the Display property in the Timeline to toggle it On.

Edge Animate shows the museumlogo1 element at 0:07 seconds.

The fade-in effect will begin at this point.

8 In the Timeline panel, turn on the Pin.

9 Drag the Pin (not the playhead) to the 0:08 second mark on the Timeline.

The playhead and the Pin separate. The playhead remains at 0:07 seconds, and a blue-colored band of arrows appears between the Pin and the playhead. The Pin represents the current state of the museumlogo1, at 100% opacity, thus you keep the playhead at the starting time and move the Pin to the ending time.

10 In the Properties panel, change the Opacity property to 0%.

Edge Animate automatically inserts a beginning and ending keyframe for the Opacity property on the Timeline. A colored band appears between the beginning and ending keyframes, indicating a smooth fade-in effect of the museumlogo1 graphic from 0% to 100% opacity.

11 Turn the Pin off and press the Spacebar on your keyboard to play the animation.

● **Note:** Sometimes you'll move the Pin when you want to really move the playhead, and vice versa, and you end up with the opposite transition, or motion. Instead of redoing the animation, you can right-click on your transition on the Timeline and choose Invert Transition from the contextual menu. Edge Animate swaps the beginning and end keyframes so your transition is reversed.

Timeline panel options

Your animation has grown to be fairly long at this point, with multiple elements on the Stage spanning 0:08 seconds, and not all of the elements fit on the Timeline. Fortunately, Edge Animate has many different display options to help you manage how you see your composition.

Zoom in and out of the Timeline

You can zoom in or out of the Timeline, depending on whether you want to see the big picture, or if you want to focus on the motion of a particular element.

Zoom Timeline Out   Zoom Timeline In

Zoom Timeline to Fit

- Click the Zoom Timeline In button on the bottom right of the Timeline panel or by pressing the equals key (=) to see more detail and smaller time increments.

- Click the Zoom Timeline Out button, the second button on the bottom left of the Timeline panel, or by pressing the minus key (–) to see less detail and larger time increments.

- Click the Zoom Timeline to Fit button on the bottom left of the Timeline panel or press the backward slash key (\) to see all your animation within the available width of the Timeline panel.

- Drag the Zoom Timeline handle between the Zoom Timeline In and Zoom Timeline Out buttons to change zoom levels smoothly.

Collapsing and hiding Timeline elements

As your composition becomes more complex, your Timeline becomes more difficult to manage because you won't be able to see all your elements. Use the Timeline options to hide and to collapse some elements in order to focus on others.

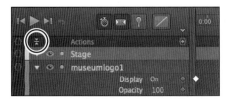

- Click the Expand/Collapse Lanes or press Shift+Ctrl+. (Windows)/ Shift+Command+ (Mac OS) to toggle between a Timeline with all the selected property lanes expanded or collapsed.

  When a property lane is collapsed, a single colored bar shows you when animation is happening. This is helpful to see the overall timing of the elements.

- Click the arrowheads in front of each element to expand or collapse the property lanes for just that element.

- Click the Only Show Animated Elements button at the bottom of the Timeline panel to hide static elements.

Show Only Animated Elements

Swapping assets

Imagine that the client for this animated banner ad calls you and tells you that they need to make a change to the exhibition information. Instead of running through the summer, the show will only run through the spring. Also, they've requested that you add a logo next to the name of the museum.

As frustrating as it is, this kind of late request isn't that unusual! You've already animated the fade-in of the museum information. What can you do now?

Fortunately, you don't have to delete your animation of the museum information and start from scratch. You can seamlessly swap one image asset with another, and the animation will proceed as before with the replacement.

Replacing an image

In the images folder in your Library panel, there is an updated image file called museumlogo2.png that the museum director has provided for you. You will replace museumlogo1.png with museumlogo2.png.

1 Select the museumlogo1 element on the Stage, Elements, or Timeline panel.

2 In the Properties panel, click the Change Image Source button located after the source path.

A list of your Library panel assets appears.

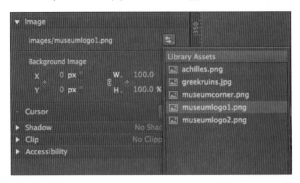

Note: Make sure that the new asset has the same dimensions as the one you want to replace. Edge Animate will keep all the properties of the original asset, including the width and height properties.

3 Select the museumlogo2.png file and click off the panel to accept the new selection.

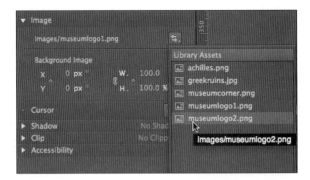

The museumlogo2.png image replaces your current image. The image now displays a silhouette of an ancient Greek vessel and the information about the timing of the exhibition has been corrected. The element name remains museumlogo1.

4 Press the spacebar to play your animation.

The museumlogo1 element appears and fades in as before, but with the replaced asset.

Copying and pasting animations

You have one final piece to add to this banner ad. At the very end of the animation, a graphic appears at the top-right corner of the Stage that tells your audience that they can buy tickets online. The image smoothly fades in, exactly like the museum logo image.

When you have elements that go through identical transitions, like this corner graphic and the museum logo, you can simply copy and paste animations to save time and effort.

Copying animation

On the Timeline, you can copy just a single property change of an element, or multiple property changes. For the museumlogo1 element, you will copy two property changes: the change in the Display property and the change in the Opacity property.

1   In the Timeline panel, select the fade-in animation of the museumlogo1 element. Hold down your Shift key and click the Display keyframe at 0:07 seconds to add it to your selection.

    The animation for the opacity change and the abrupt change in Display property are selected.

Note: You can also simply click on the top colored bar of an element and all of the property lanes under it will become selected.

2   Right-click and choose Copy from the contextual menu that appears.

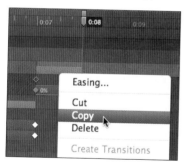

The selected animations are copied.

Pasting animation

Next, you'll paste the animation onto a new element. The new element will undergo all the same transitions that have been copied.

1   Drag the museumcorner.png image asset from the Library panel onto the Stage, and use the Smart Guides to position it at the top-right corner of the Stage.

A new element called museumcorner appears in the Timeline and Elements panel.

2   If the museumcorner element isn't at the top of the Elements stack, drag it to the top so it overlaps all the other elements.

3   Now you need to decide at what point in time you want to paste the animation to the museumcorner element. Move the playhead to 0:08.500 seconds.

The position of the playhead determines where on the Timeline the animation is pasted.

Note: You can also access the Paste command from the top menu. Choose Edit > Paste or press Ctrl+V (Windows)/ Command+V (Mac OS) to paste.

4   Right-click on the museumcorner element on the Stage, Timeline, or Elements panel and choose Paste from the contextual menu.

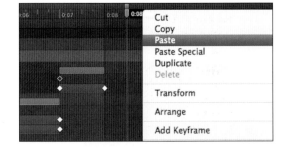

Edge Animate pastes the Display keyframe and keyframes for Opacity onto the museumlogo element at 0:08.500 seconds.

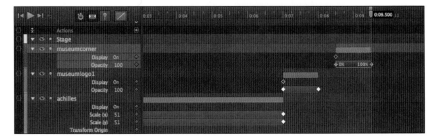

5   Press the spacebar to play your animation.

The corner graphic goes through the same fade-in animation as does the museum logo.

Special paste options

Edge Animate provides four special paste options for greater control over how the copied animations are applied. When you right-click to paste an animation, you can choose the Paste Special option, which has Paste Transitions To Location, Paste Transitions From Location, Paste Inverted, and Paste All.

- **Paste Transitions To Location** is the default paste behavior. This option pastes all the copied transitions so the transitions *end* at the current target. For example, say that you copied an animation of a box moving from X=0 to X=100 pixels. You select a circle at X=150 and choose Paste Transitions To Location. The resulting paste moves the circle from X=50 to X=150. The circle moves 100 pixels and ends at its current position.

- **Paste Transitions From Location** (Shift+Ctrl+V [Windows]/Shift+Command+V [Mac OS]) pastes all the copied transitions so the transitions *start* at the current target. For example, say that you copied an animation of a box moving from X=0 to X=100 pixels. You select a circle at X=150 and choose Paste Transitions From Location. The resulting paste moves the circle from X=150 to X=250. The circle moves 100 pixels starting from its current position.

- **Paste Inverted** pastes all the copied transitions so the transitions *end* at the current target, and then reverses the direction. For example, say that you copied an animation of a box moving from X=0 to X=100 pixels. You select a circle at X=150 and choose Paste Inverted. The resulting paste moves the circle from X=250 to X=150. The circle moves 100 pixels *to the left* and ends at its current position.

- **Paste All** pastes the transitions and the original element, so you end up with a duplicate on the Timeline panel. You can also simply choose Edit > Duplicate, press Ctrl+D (Windows)/Command+D (Mac OS), or right-click and choose Duplicate, which will create a duplicate element along with its animation. The difference between Paste All and Duplicate is that Paste All allows you to paste the duplicate at a different point in time. Duplicate makes an exact copy of elements, animation, and timing.

Adding easing to refine motion

Your banner ad is nearly complete. All the elements are in place on the Stage, and you've incorporated eye-catching motion and smooth transitions. However, there is more you can do to make the animation even better: add easing.

About easing

Easing refers to the way in which an animation proceeds. When easing refers to motion (the change in position), think of it as acceleration or deceleration. An element that moves from one side of the Stage to the other side can start off slowly, then build up momentum, and then stop suddenly. Or, the object can start off quickly, and then gradually come to a halt.

But easing can also be more complicated. It can describe motion that oscillates, bounces, and does other complex patterns. Your keyframes indicate the beginning and ending values of a property, and easing determines how your element gets from one to the other.

Without easing, animation proceeds in a *linear* fashion. That means that there is the same amount of change at every time interval. For example, your animation of the title moves an equal amount of pixels every second. If you graph the time of the animation on the horizontal axis with the amount of change (in distance) on the vertical axis, you'd see a straight line, as follows:

If the title were to start moving slowly, and gradually get up to speed, then the first few time intervals would show very small changes in distance. The graph would be curved, with a flattened portion at its beginning, like the bright white line here. This kind of ease is known as an *ease-in*.

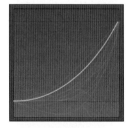

If the title were to start moving normally but gradually slow down, then the last few time intervals would show increasingly smaller changes in distance. The graph would also be curved, but with a flattened portion at the end, like the bright white line here. This kind of ease is known as an *ease-out*.

Easing can be best seen with motion (changes in position, scale, or rotation), but you can apply easing to any kind of animation. The effect is often subtle, but can make animation appear more natural and make objects move with a sense of weight.

Adding an ease-out to motion

You'll modify the linear motion of the title to make it slowly ease to a stop.

1 Select the title1 element in the Timeline.

The Left property transition becomes selected.

2 Click the Easing option on the Timeline, or right-click the animation span and choose Easing from the contextual menu.

The Easing menu appears. The first column lists all the types of eases available. The options in the first column determine what part of the animation is affected (the start, end, or both the start and end).

3 Select Ease Out.

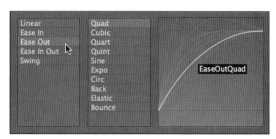

The Ease Out option affects the end of the motion. A list of curves appears in the second column, with their graphical depiction in the third column. The different curves represent the severity of the ease out.

4 Select the Quad option.

The Quad option provides the least amount of easing. The Quad graph highlights to show you the curvature of the ease graph.

5 Click out of the Easing menu to close it.

The ease is applied to the title animation. The Easing icon displays the EaseOutQuad curve.

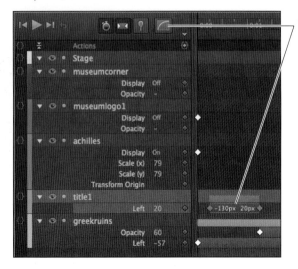

The Easing icon identifies the type of easing for selected transition

6 Press the spacebar to play the animation.

The effect is subtle, but the title animation gradually slows down as it reaches its destination.

7 Click the Easing option again, and select Ease Out > Quint. Click out of the Easing menu to close it.

The Easing icon displays the EaseOutQuint curve, which has a more dramatic slowdown. How different is the ease-out of the motion of the title?

8 Experiment with the different Easing options. In particular, try out Ease Out > Elastic and Ease Out > Bounce.

With Elastic and Bounce, the title oscillates when it reaches its destination, simulating the elasticity of a rubber band or the decreasing bounces of a ball.

Adding an ease-out to a change of scale

You'll modify the linear scaling of the image of Achilles to make it slowly ease in to its final size.

1 Select all the animated properties for the achilles element.

The Scale (x) and Scale (y) animation becomes selected.

2 Click the Easing option on the Timeline, or right-click the animation span and choose Easing from the contextual menu.

The Easing menu appears.

3 Select Ease Out.

4 Select the Quint option.

The Quint option provides a strong amount of easing.

5 Click out of the Easing menu to close it.

The ease is applied to the Achilles scaling animation. The Easing icon displays the EaseOutQuint curve.

6 Press the spacebar to play the animation.

The image of Achilles pops into view suddenly and dramatically, and as the camera seems to pull away (and the statue gets smaller), the animation gradually slows.

Note: You can apply different kinds of easing to different animations of the same element. For example, an element could have one kind of easing for its change in opacity and another kind of easing for its motion.

Editing overall timing

Earlier in this lesson, you moved keyframes and animation spans, and added time to play with pacing and the synchronization of elements. When the animation is nearly done, as it is now, it's useful to revisit the overall timing. Often, it's not until you see all the elements together that you can get a sense of which graphics need to remain on the Stage a little longer, or whether some transitions need to overlap to provide a better sense of cohesion.

Modifying the total length

When you select all the animated elements in the Timeline panel, you can change the total animation length while maintaining the same timing among the individual elements.

1 Click and drag your mouse cursor over all the elements in your Timeline, or simply click inside the Timeline panel and choose Edit > Select All or press Ctrl+A (Windows)/Command+A (Mac OS).

All the elements of your Edge Animate composition are selected.

2   Move your mouse cursor close to the right edge of the last animated element.

Your cursor changes to a double-headed arrow, indicating that you can move the selection.

3   Click and drag all the selected elements back to 0:07 seconds.

Your entire animation shortens to 0:07 seconds, with the individual animated elements shortening in proportion.

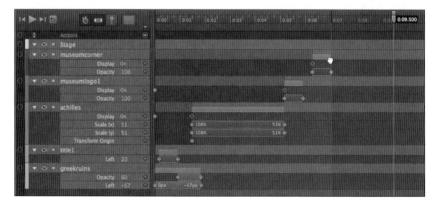

4   Press the spacebar to play the animation.

The banner ad plays within a shorter time frame, which is a little more effective at getting to the point.

Editing selected animations

After studying your animation, you may find that it still needs to move quicker. But you only want some portions to move quicker, while maintaining the length of others. Shift-click to select multiple elements, or use the Lock option and Select All to select unprotected (unlocked) elements.

1 *Do one of the following:*

- Click and drag your cursor over the achilles, museumlogo1, and museumcorner animated elements.

- Hold down your Shift key and select the achilles, museumlogo1, and the museumcorner animated elements.

- Lock the greekruins and title1 elements, then choose Edit > Select All or press Ctrl+A (Windows) or Command+A (Mac OS).

2 Move your mouse cursor close to the right edge of the last animated element.

Your cursor changes to a double-headed arrow, indicating that you can move the selection.

3 Click and drag the selected elements back to 0:06 seconds.

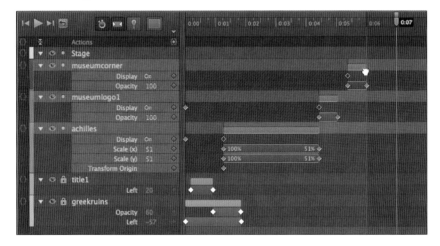

The selected animation shortens to end at 0:06 seconds, with the individual animated elements shortening in proportion. The unselected animation (greekruins and the title1 elements) remains undisturbed.

4 Unlock the greekruins element, if you had previously locked it.

5 Move your mouse cursor over the last keyframes for its Left and Opacity property.

Your cursor changes to a double-headed arrow, indicating that you can move the keyframes.

6 Click and drag the keyframes forward to the point where the statue of Achilles ends its scale change.

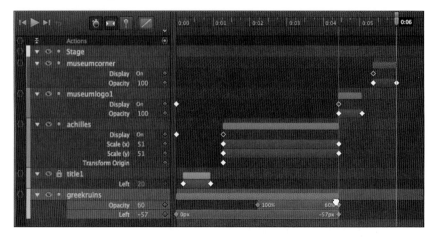

The slow panning motion and fade-out of the greekruins element now continues while the image of Achilles bursts onto the Stage. The overlap of animations help provide more continuity throughout the banner ad.

Your animated banner ad for the museum is complete!

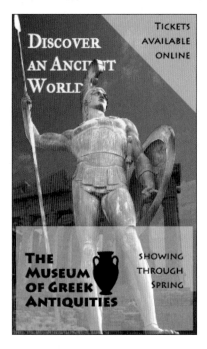

Review questions

1 How are the Pin and playhead used to create an animation?

2 What happens when you change a property of an element when Auto-Keyframe mode is enabled but Auto-Transition mode is disabled?

3 How do you change the origin of transformation of an element?

4 How do you make an element suddenly appear on the Stage at a later point in the Timeline?

5 What is easing, and how do you apply it to an animation?

Review answers

1 The Pin works by "pinning," or fixing, the current values of your element. You can then move the playhead to a different position on the Timeline and change the properties of your element. Edge Animate will create the keyframes to animate *from* the Pin *to* the playhead. Use the Pin and playhead to create the beginning and ending keyframes of an animation in a single edit.

2 When Auto-Keyframe mode is enabled, Edge Animate automatically creates property keyframes for changes to an element on the Stage. When Auto-Transition mode is enabled, Edge Animate automatically creates smooth transitions between keyframes. So, if Auto-Keyframe mode is enabled but Auto-Transition mode is disabled, then changes in an element's property will result in abrupt visual changes.

3 To change the origin of transformation of an element, choose the Transform tool and select the element. Click and drag the centerpoint, which represents the default origin of transformation to a new location. You can also change the values of the Origin X and Origin Y in the Transform section of the Properties panel.

4 To make an element appear suddenly on the Stage at a later point in the Timeline, you create different keyframes for its Display property. On the initial keyframe, the Display property is Off so the element is not visible. On a later keyframe, the Display property is On so the element is visible.

5 Easing refers to the way in which an animation proceeds. Easing is the rate of change of an element's property. To apply a different ease, select an animation in the Timeline and click the Easing options to select an ease curve. An Ease In affects the beginning of the motion, and an Ease Out affects the end of the motion. An Ease In Out affects both the beginning and end of the motion. To disable an ease, choose the Linear option.

4 REFINING ANIMATION AND ADDING COMPLEXITY

Lesson Overview

In this lesson, you'll learn how to do the following:

- Create Symbols
- Use Symbols for nested animation
- Edit Symbols
- Add a trigger to create a looping animation
- Understand instances
- Insert different playback commands for instances
- Import and export Symbols
- Animate with the Clip property
- Incorporate drop shadows
- Use advanced eases to refine motion

 This lesson will take about three hours to complete. Open the Lesson04 folder from the lesson files to begin.

Learn about Symbols to create complex, nested animations and use clipping and shadows to add more dramatic effects to your compositions.

Getting started

In this lesson, you'll dig deeper into animation and learn more advanced techniques such as creating symbols for nested animations and using clipping for sophisticated visual effects. You'll also apply easing curves that can create interesting and realistic motion.

1   Choose File > Open or click the Open File link from the Getting Started opening panel. In the Open dialog box, select the 04End.an file in the Lesson04/04End folder and click Open to see the final project.

2   Choose File > Preview in Browser or press Ctrl+Enter (Windows)/ Command+Return (Mac OS).

Edge Animate creates the necessary files to display the final animation in your default browser, which opens automatically. The browser shows an animated introduction for a website for a fictional new television series. The opening photo of a crime scene is quickly dissected by yellow caution tape. Three main characters emerge from the bottom edge of the Stage and the title of the television series unravels from another caution tape. Finally, several fictional reviews bounce in from the right.

3   Close the browser.

4   In Edge Animate, choose File > New or press Ctrl+N (Windows)/Command+N (Mac OS) to start a new document.

5   In the Properties panel, change the Stage size to 1000 pixels wide and 650 pixels high, which will be your final animation size. Leave the Stage color as white (#ffffff). Since the Stage for this project is so wide, you can close the Lessons panel to make more room.

6 In the Composition ID field at the top of the Properties panel, name your Edge Animate composition **Police Line: Do Not Cross**.

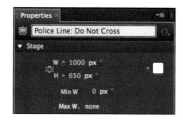

7 Save your file as **04_workingcopy** in the 04Start folder.

8 The 04Start folder contains an images folder that contains all the necessary image assets to build this animation. The images folder shows up in the Assets folder of your Library panel in Edge Animate.

9 Drag the background.jpg file from the images folder in the Library panel onto the Stage and position it at X=0, Y=0.

10 Lock the background element.

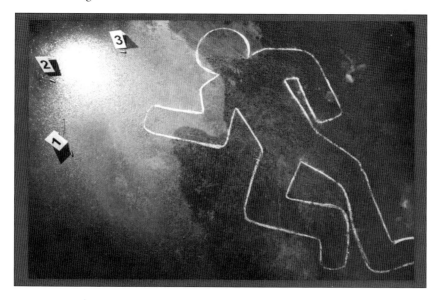

About symbols

Symbols are a special kind of asset that is created in Edge Animate and saved inside the Library panel in its own folder, called Symbols.

Symbols are used to group together elements with an independent timeline. This allows the elements to have their own animation separate from the animation that is happening on the main Timeline. For example, an animation of a car would be best depicted as a collection of connected graphics with coordinated movement—the front and back wheels rotate as the body and wheels move across the Stage. If the car body and the wheels are converted to a symbol, you can animate the rotation of the wheels inside the car symbol. You can then animate the entire symbol of the car across the Stage as a single unit, and the wheels will continue to turn independently of the car's motion on the Stage.

Adobe Flash Professional users will be familiar with the concept of symbols with independent timelines. In Flash Professional, the MovieClip symbol is most like the symbol in Edge Animate.

Symbols allow you to create more complicated animations, such as a butterfly moving across the Stage as the wings flap up and down, or an animation of the constant motion of gears in the background. Symbols enable *nested* animations—internal animations of elements, each independent of the other and independent of the animation happening on the main Timeline.

Creating nested animations

In the animated opener for this television series, two rolls of caution tape roll across the Stage, unfurling two yellow ribbons. Look carefully at the animation again, and you can see that the rolls of tape rotate as they move across the Stage. The rolls of tape contain nested animations. The rolls of tape are symbols. The symbols contain an animation of the roll rotating, and the symbols themselves simply move across the main Stage (change in X and Y positions).

Converting elements to symbols

You'll begin building this animation by creating the symbols for the rolls of tape.

1 Expand the images folder within the Assets section of the Library panel.

   The image files in the images folder appear.

2 Drag the backroll.png file from the Library onto the Stage.

3 Drag the frontroll.png file from the Library onto the Stage.

4 Position the frontroll element so that the bottom edge of the backroll element aligns with the middle of the frontroll element.

The roll of tape is complete. The roll of tape is constructed in separate pieces so the front can be animated easily.

5 Select both the frontroll and the backroll element.

6 Choose Modify > Convert to Symbol, or press Ctrl+Y (Windows)/Command+Y (Mac OS). You can also right-click the selections and choose Convert to Symbol from the popup menu.

The Create Symbol dialog box appears.

7 In the Symbol Name field, enter **rolloftape**. Keep the Autoplay timeline option checked, and click OK.

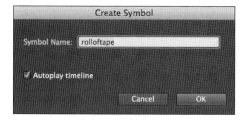

The frontroll and backroll elements are converted to a symbol called rolloftape, which is saved in the Library panel in the Symbols folder.

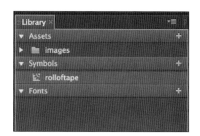

The symbol called rolloftape appears on the Timeline and the Elements panel. Your symbol is a single element, which you can move around the Stage and make transformations, which would affect both the frontroll and backroll components.

A Playback option appears on the Timeline under the rolloftape symbol. There's no animation within your rolloftape symbol (yet), so the Playback options aren't relevant at this point in time.

Creating animations inside Symbols

You'll animate the front face of the roll of tape rotating, and the animation will be created *inside* the symbol.

1   Double-click the rolloftape symbol on the Stage or in the Elements panel, or select the rolloftape symbol and choose Modify > Edit Symbol. You can also right-click the selection and choose Edit Symbol "rolloftape" from the popup menu.

The Stage dims and you enter Symbol editing mode, where you have access to the elements that make up your symbol. At the top of the Stage, the name of the symbol, rolloftape, appears as a reminder that you are no longer on the main Stage, but are editing a symbol.

Name of symbol currently being edited

On the Timeline and the Elements panel, the frontroll and backroll elements appear.

2   Select the frontroll element and activate the Pin on the Timeline.

The Pin turns blue, indicating that it is activated.

3   Drag the playhead on the Timeline to 0:01 seconds.

The playhead and the Pin separate. The Pin remains at 0:00 seconds, and a gold-colored band of arrows appears between the Pin and the playhead.

4   In the Properties panel, change the Rotate property to 360 degrees.

Edge Animate creates a beginning keyframe at 0:00 seconds for a Rotate of 0 degrees and an ending keyframe at 0:01 seconds for a Rotate of 360 degrees.

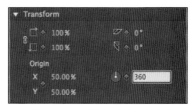

5   Click on the Pin to turn it off.

6   Press the spacebar.

Edge Animate previews the animation. The front face of the roll of tape rotates one full rotation.

Exiting Symbol editing mode

Your animation inside your symbol is done for now. Return to the main Stage to continue working on the animation.

1   Double-click on a part of the Stage outside your symbol, or click on the Stage link at the upper-left corner of the Stage.

The main Stage returns (and is no longer dimmed), and the main Elements and Timeline panel return.

The rolloftape symbol on the Timeline displays a series of gray arrows within its Playback lane that lasts for 1 second. This represents the duration of its internal animation. You can see how long the animation inside the symbol lasts in relation to the animation of elements on the main Timeline.

2   Press the spacebar.

Edge Animate previews the animation. The front face of the roll of tape rotates one full rotation.

Animating symbols on the Stage

You can animate symbols in the same manner as any other element. Use the Pin and playhead to create keyframes to establish when properties change over a period of time.

Creating the ribbon

As the roll of tape moves across the Stage, it stretches a yellow ribbon behind it. You'll add the yellow ribbon as a simple rectangular element and animate it by simply changing its Size properties.

1   Make sure that your playhead is at 0:00 seconds.

2   Select the Rectangle tool, and change the background color to yellow (#fff600).

3 Create a rectangle on the Stage, and modify the Size so that it is W=200 pixels and H=90 pixels.

A rectangular shape appears on the Stage for the ribbon.

4 Rename the newly created Rectangle element **ribbon**.

Transforming the symbol

The rolloftape symbol was created with its front face as a perfect circle to make animating its rotation easy. But it'll be more realistic for the roll of tape to appear at a slight angle. You can make transformations to the symbol, and the nested animation and all the elements within the symbol will be affected proportionately.

1 On the Timeline, turn off Auto-Keyframe Mode.

2 Select the rolloftape symbol.

3 Change the Scale property so the vertical dimension (scaleY) is at 80%. Make sure that the Link Scale option is off so the horizontal and vertical Scale properties are *not* kept constant.

The symbol becomes squished, and the front face of the roll of tape appears as an ellipse.

4 Drag the rolloftape symbol in the Elements panel above the ribbon element so it overlaps the ribbon element on the Stage.

5 Select both the rolloftape symbol and the ribbon element and choose Modify > Align > Bottom.

The ribbon and the roll of tape are now positioned to appear as a single object.

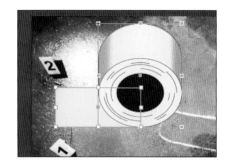

Rotating two elements around a common center point

Next, you'll rotate the ribbon and the roll so the animation can proceed in a more dynamic diagonal motion across the stage. You can select and rotate multiple elements, but they will rotate around their own center points. Change the X and Y coordinates of the Transform Origin property so the elements share a common point of transformation and rotate together.

1 Select both the ribbon and the rolloftape elements.

2 Select the Transform Tool and rotate the selection.

Notice how both elements rotate together, but each of them rotates around its own center point.

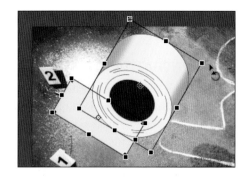

3 Press Ctrl+Z (Windows) or Command+Z (Mac OS) to undo the rotation.

4 With the Transform Tool still selected, drag the transformation origin point of the rolloftape symbol and move it on top of the transformation origin point of the ribbon element.

The points should snap to each other. The origins of transformation for both elements are now identical.

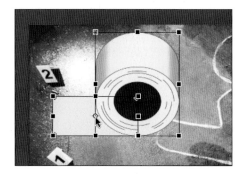

5 Rotate both elements so the Rotate property is at −23 degrees.

The ribbon and roll of tape rotate together.

6 Move both elements off the Stage at the lower-left corner.

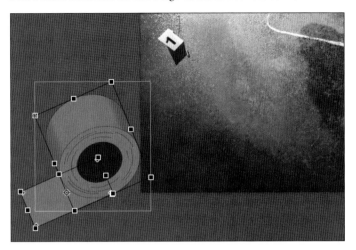

Animating the ribbon and the roll

The roll of tape will move from the bottom left to the top right of the Stage at the same time that the ribbon changes its width.

1 Activate the Pin on the Timeline.

The Pin turns blue and Auto-Keyframe mode automatically turns on.

2 Drag the playhead on the Timeline to 0:02 seconds and the Pin to 0:00 seconds.

The playhead and the Pin separate. A gold-colored band of arrows appears between the Pin and the playhead.

3 With the Selection tool selected, select the ribbon element and drag its right edge to extend its width all the way past the Stage on the far right-hand side. You can also change the Size property in the Properties panel so W=1550 pixels.

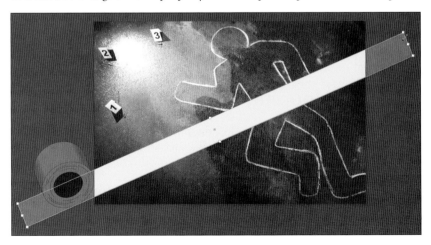

4 Drag the rolloftape symbol to the far side of the Stage so it remains with the stretched-out ribbon. The position of the rolloftape element should be about X=986, Y=−124.

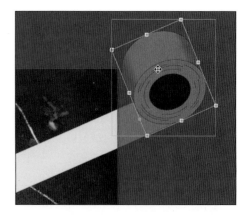

Edge Animate creates the beginning and ending keyframes for the ribbon element with changes to its Width, Left, and Top properties. Keyframes for the rolloftape element with changes to its Left and Top properties are also created.

5 Turn off the Pin and press the spacebar.

The roll of tape moves across the Stage, leaving behind a yellow ribbon. As the roll of tape moves, it rotates.

Watch carefully, however, and you'll notice that the rotation of the tape stops at 0:01 seconds. Your nested animation lasts only 1 second, while the animation on the main Timeline goes for 2 seconds. You'll need to extend the nested animation so it lasts longer.

A simple solution is to create a loop so the nested animation plays continuously. You'll do that next.

Creating a looping animation

A *loop* is a continuous animation. When the animation reaches its end, it loops back to the beginning. If the beginning keyframe and ending keyframes are identical, then the loop is seamless.

To create a looping animation within your rolloftape symbol, you'll add a trigger. A trigger is a simple command that tells Edge Animate to do something when the playhead reaches a certain point on the Timeline. You'll learn more about triggers and adding code, in general, in the next lesson.

Adding a trigger to a symbol timeline

You can add triggers to any Timeline, but to make your nested animation loop, you add the trigger to the timeline of a symbol.

1   Edit your rolloftape symbol by double-clicking it on the Stage.

All other elements on the Stage dim, and you enter Symbol editing mode.

2   Move your playhead to the end of the animation at 0:01 seconds.

3   In the Timeline panel, click the Insert Trigger button on the top Actions row. You can also choose Timeline > Insert Trigger or press Ctrl+T (Windows)/ Command+T (Mac OS).

An icon that appears as a diamond enclosed by curly braces appears on the Timeline at 0:01 seconds. The icon represents a trigger.

A panel appears with a large white text-entry field and a column of code snippet options on the right-hand side. The panel is titled Trigger@1000ms, referring to the trigger's position at 1,000 milliseconds, or 1 seconds.

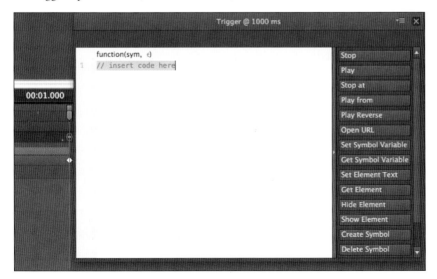

4 Put your cursor at the end of the existing script and press Enter (Windows) or return (Mac OS) to create a new line.

The current script, `//insert code here`, is known as a *comment*. Comments always begin with two backslash characters, and are descriptions of the code. Comments are non-functional, and don't add significantly to the file size of your composition.

5 From the menu of code snippets on the right side of the panel, select the Play from option.

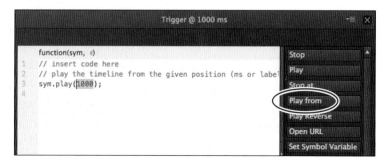

New code appears in the panel. The new code comes with its own comments that describe its function. The code, `sym.play(1000);`, moves the playhead to a particular point in time on the Timeline and begins playing.

6 Replace the 1000 within the parentheses in the code with **0**.

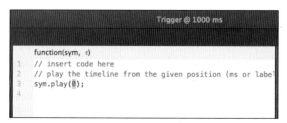

The number in between the parentheses of the `play()` command represents the time to which the playhead will move. Since you want the playhead to move to the beginning of the Timeline at 0:00 seconds, enter 0 in the parentheses of the `play()` command.

7 Close the panel and return to the main Stage.

The gray arrows in the Playback lane of the rolloftape symbol remain 1 second long, and previewing the animation within Edge Animate doesn't display the looping animation within the symbol.

However, when you preview the composition in a browser by choosing File > Preview in Browser, or pressing Ctrl+Enter (Windows)/Command+Enter

Mac OS), you'll see the animation of the roll of tape looping, and rotating for the entire duration of its travel across the Stage.

Symbol instances

The value of symbols reaches beyond the fact that you can create nested animations. Symbols allow you to easily place multiple *instances* of them on the Stage. An instance is a single element of the symbol definition in the Library. You can have multiple instances, which makes creating and editing complex animations simple. Each instance can be modified slightly on the main Stage, creating many variations of one Symbol.

For example, for this splash screen, you'll add another roll of tape rolling across the Stage in the opposite direction, but you won't have to create an entirely new animation or symbol. You can use the same rolloftape symbol in your Library, and simply make a transformation to flip the instance horizontally. The roll of tape will animate for the second instance in the opposite direction.

Adding additional symbol instances

You'll add a second instance of the rolloftape symbol on the Stage to create the animation of the ribbon stretching in the opposite direction.

1   Move your playhead back to 0:00 seconds, and turn off Auto-Keyframe mode.

2   Expand the Symbols folder in the Library panel and drag the rolloftape symbol onto the Stage.

A second instance of the rolloftape symbol appears on the Stage, Elements, and Timeline panel. The second instance is automatically named rolloftape2.

3 Press the spacebar to preview the animation.

Your first roll of tape moves across the Stage, and rotates as it does so. Your second roll of tape also rotates. The animations of the two instances are in synchrony because they reference the same symbol definition in the Library.

Transforming the second symbol instance

You'll use the Transform tool to flip the symbol instance horizontally to make the rotation of the front face of the roll of tape go in the opposite direction.

1 Choose the Transform tool and click on the second symbol instance, the rolloftape2 element.

2 Drag the control points on the top or bottom side of the bounding box to squash the instance the same amount as the first instance. Make the same 80% scaleY transformation as the first instance.

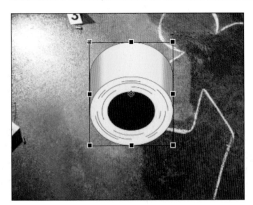

3 Drag the control points on the left or right side of the bounding box to squash the instance in the other direction. Keep dragging the bounding box past its center point so it flips.

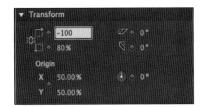

The scaleX Transform property in the Properties panel should display negative values. Make the scaleX property –100%.

4 Press the spacebar to preview the animation.

The second instance of the symbol rotates in the opposite direction of the first instance.

Adding the second animation

The next step is a repeat of the first animation. You'll add a yellow rectangle for the ribbon (you can copy and paste the first one you created), and you'll animate the ribbon changing its width, and the instance changing its position.

1   Copy and paste the ribbon element.

    The new ribbon element is automatically named ribbonCopy. Rename it
    ribbon2.

2   Modify the ribbon2 element so the width is 200 pixels, the height is 90 pixels, and the rotation is 6 degrees.

3   In the Elements panel, drag the ribbon2 element under the rolloftape2 element.

    The rolloftape2 element overlaps the ribbon2 element.

4   Position both the rolloftape2 and the ribbon2 elements on the bottom right of the Stage. The rolloftape2 element should be positioned at X=775, Y=347. The ribbon2 element should be positioned at X=838, Y=486.

5   Activate the Pin on the Timeline.

    The Pin turns blue and Auto-Keyframe mode automatically turns on.

6   Drag the Pin to 0:02 seconds and the playhead to 0:03 seconds.

    The playhead and the Pin separate. The starting point for the animation is set for 0:02 seconds and the ending point is set for 0:03 seconds.

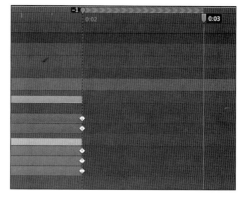

7 With the Selection tool, select the ribbon element and drag its left edge to extend its width all the way past the Stage on the far-left side. The width of the ribbon2 element should be W=1200 pixels.

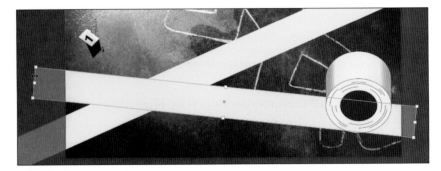

8 Drag the rolloftape2 element to the far-left side of the Stage so it remains with the stretched-out ribbon. The position should be X=−196, Y=241.

Edge Animate creates the beginning and ending keyframes for the ribbon2 and rolloftape2 elements with changes to Left, Top, and Width properties.

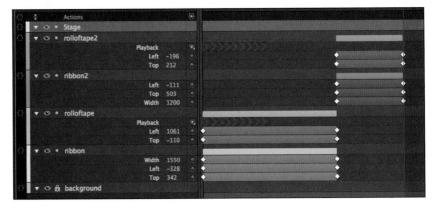

9 Turn off the Pin and press the spacebar.

The first roll of tape moves from left to right in the first 2 seconds. The second roll of tape, which begins on the Stage, moves in the opposite direction as soon as the first animation ends.

However, the second roll of tape rotates even before it begins to move, creating an unrealistic effect. You want the roll of tape to remain still, and only begin to rotate at 0:02 seconds when it unrolls the ribbon.

You can control when the nested animation of a symbol instance plays by using the Playback options. You'll do that next.

Playback commands

The default behavior for symbol instances is to play all nested animations, which you can see on the Timeline as the band of gray arrows in the Playback lane of your Symbol. The band of gray arrows represents the duration of the nested animation.

However, you can change the default playback behavior with Playback commands. You can stop, play, play in reverse, or choose exact times to play your nested animation. You set the Playback options for *each* symbol instance, so individual instances of the same symbol can play their animations differently.

Stopping a nested animation

For your second roll of tape, you'll change its Playback option so its animation is prevented from playing.

1 On the Timeline, move the playhead to 0:00 seconds.

2 Click on the Playback options for your rolloftape2 element, and choose Stop.

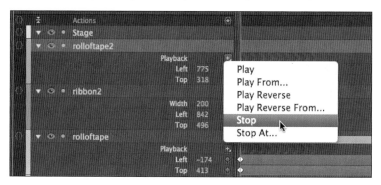

A stop icon appears on the Playback lane of the rolloftape2 element, which prevents its animation from playing at 0:00 seconds. The band of gray arrows disappears from the Timeline.

3   Press the spacebar to preview your animation, or press Ctrl+Enter (Windows)/ Command+return (Mac OS) to preview it in a browser.

The nested animation inside the rolloftape2 element does not play.

Playing a nested animation

Although you managed to stop the animation of the second roll of tape, you want it to begin playing at 0:02 seconds, when it moves across the Stage. You can add a new Playback command at any point along the Timeline.

1   On the Timeline, move the playhead to 0:02 seconds.

2   Click on the Playback options for your rolloftape2 element, and choose Play.

Note: Explore the other, more advanced Playback commands, such as Play From, Play Reverse, Play Reverse From, or Stop At. These options give you control over the precise time at which to stop or play the symbol animation, or to play the animation in reverse.

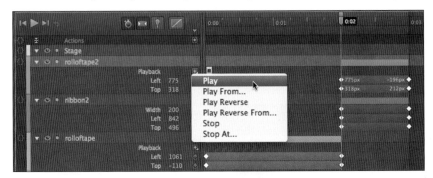

A play icon appears on the Playback lane of the rolloftape2 element. The band of gray arrows appears at 0:02 seconds after the play icon.

3   Press the spacebar to preview your animation, or press Ctrl+Enter (Windows)/
    Command+return (Mac OS) to preview it in a browser.

    The Playback commands for the rolloftape2 element coordinate its nested
    animation with the animation on the main Timeline. The Playback instructions
    stop the rotation of the roll of tape until the playhead on the main Timeline
    reaches 0:02 seconds.

Editing Playback commands

Editing Playback commands is a straightforward matter.

- To delete a Playback command, select it and press the Delete key.

- To move a Playback command to a different time, click and drag it along
  the Timeline.

- To delete *all* Playback commands for an instance, select the Playback lane on
  the Timeline and press the Delete key.

    Edge Animate deletes all the Playback commands, reverting the instance to
    the default playback option, which is to automatically play its animation at
    0:00 seconds.

Editing symbols

You have two ways of editing symbols. You've already seen how you can double-
click a symbol on the Stage to edit it. You added the nested animation of the front
face of the roll of tape rotating this way.

The second way to edit a symbol is to double-click the symbol icon in the Library
panel. Edge Animate provides you with a symbol-editing environment clear of
other Stage elements, so you can make edits without distractions.

When making edits to symbols, you'll see your changes reflected in all instances of
the symbol on the Stage.

Modifying the graphics for the roll of tape

Suppose the client for this animated television series website is not pleased with the look of the roll of tape. She thinks the concentric circles around the hole are too dark and sharp, and wants you to soften their appearance. Luckily, you can easily edit Symbols to make global changes to all the instances on the Stage.

1   In the Library panel, double-click the icon in front of the rolloftape symbol.

    Edge Animate takes you to symbol-editing mode for your rolloftape symbol. The Stage displays only the graphics and animation for your symbol.

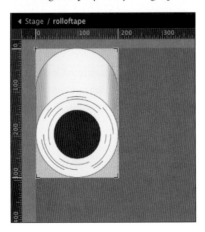

2   Select the image of the front of the roll of tape, called frontroll.

3   In the Properties panel, click the Change Image Source button.

    A popup window displays all of the Library panel Assets.

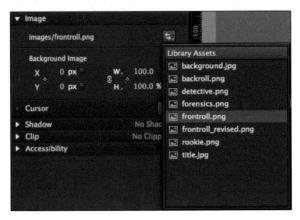

4 Choose the frontroll_revised.png file as the replacement, and click outside the popup window to dismiss it.

The frontroll_revised.png file replaces the existing image file. The symbol now shows the same animation of the roll of tape, but with softer, slightly blurred, striations.

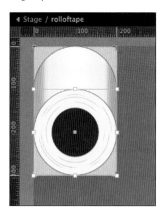

5 Exit symbol-editing mode by clicking on the Stage link on the upper-left corner of the Stage, or by double-clicking on an empty part of the Stage.

Edge Animate updates both instances of your rolloftape symbol automatically to show the revised graphic.

Symbol options

Delete and duplicate symbols directly from the Library panel.

- To delete a symbol in the Library, select it and press the Delete key.

  If there are instances of your symbol on the Stage, Edge Animate alerts you. All instances will be deleted if their reference in the Library is deleted.

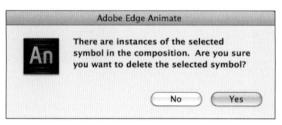

- To duplicate a symbol, right-click on it in the Library and choose Duplicate.

  Edge Animate creates a duplicate symbol in the Library with a new name.

Sharing symbols

You can copy and paste symbols between Edge Animate files, but it can get cumbersome if you need to share many symbols between developers working on common projects. Edge Animate provides an easy way to export and import symbols. Select a symbol or multiple symbols in your Library panel and right-click to choose Export. You can save your selected symbols in a single, separate file, called an Edge Animate Symbol file, that has the extension .ansym.

To import an Edge Animate Symbol file into a new composition, click the Add Symbol button next to the Symbols folder of your Library panel. Choose Import Symbols, and select the Edge Animate Symbol file. All the symbols and their dependent image assets (such as the JPG or PNG files) will be imported into your Edge Animate composition.

Adding the characters

Next, you'll add the three main characters for this television series website: the rookie, the detective, and the forensics expert. They'll emerge from the bottom of the Stage, just after the second roll of tape finishes its animation.

Add the images

The three characters are provided for you as PNG files in the images folder in the Library.

1   In the Library panel, expand the images folder, and drag the rookie.png, forensics.png, and detective.png files to the Stage.

2   In the Elements panel, rearrange the elements so the rookie overlaps the forensics, and the forensics overlaps the detective.

3   Position the rookie element at X=386, Y=647. Position the forensics element at X=28, Y=647. Position the detective element at X=661, Y=647.

The initial positions of the three characters are below the Stage.

Animate the images

You'll create a simple change in position to introduce the three characters.

1   Activate the Pin on the Timeline.

The Pin turns blue and Auto-Keyframe mode automatically turns on.

2   Drag the Pin to 0:03 seconds and the playhead to 0:04 seconds.

The playhead and the Pin separate. The starting point for the animation is set for 0:03 seconds and the ending point is set for 0:04 seconds.

3 Drag all three characters upward on the Stage.

4 Position the forensics element at Y=220. Position the rookie element at Y=66. Position the detective element at Y=59. Their bottom edges should line up with the bottom edge of the Stage.

Edge Animate creates the beginning and ending keyframes for the three characters with changes to their Top properties.

5 Turn off the Pin and press the spacebar.

After the yellow caution tape unravels across the Stage in both directions, the forensics expert, the rookie, and the detective rise from the bottom of the Stage.

Clipping animation

The Clip property of an element controls how much of the graphic is visible. You can use the Clip property to crop the element's top, bottom, left, or right sides. You can animate the Clip values to achieve interesting effects. For example, you can animate the clipping of a view out a window to make it appear as if the window is opening or closing, and revealing or hiding the view. You can simulate a cinematic transition known as a wipe by using clipping animation.

In the next addition to your composition, you'll add the last yellow caution banner, which contains the main title. You'll animate the Clip property of the image so the banner is slowly revealed from left to right.

Add the title banner

The title banner is provided for you in the images folder in the Library panel.

1   In the Library panel, expand the images folder, and drag the title.jpg image to the Stage.

2   In the Elements panel, drag the title element so it lies under all the other elements, but overlaps the background.

3   Position the title element at X=0, Y=20.

The banner appears near the top of the Stage behind the characters' heads.

Changing the clip property

You can control the clipping of any element with either the Clipping tool or the Clip properties in the Properties panel.

1   Activate the Pin on the Timeline.

The Pin turns blue and Auto-Keyframe mode automatically turns on.

2 Drag the Pin to 0:05 seconds and the playhead to 0:04 seconds.

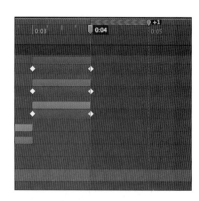

The playhead and the Pin separate. The starting point for the animation is set for 0:04 seconds and the ending point, with the banner in full view, is set for 0:05 seconds.

3 Select the Clipping tool (C) in the Tools panel.

4 Select the title element.

A green boundary box with control points on the edges and corners appears around the title element.

5 Click and drag the control point on the right edge of the bounding box to the left until it reaches the left edge and completely collapses.

In the Properties panel, you can see the Clip values of the top, left, right, and bottom edges. The right edge should be at 0 pixels.

Edge Animate clips the title banner completely, so nothing of the image is visible. Edge Animate displays a ghosted pattern where the image is clipped.

6 Turn off the Pin and press the spacebar.

Edge Animate creates a beginning keyframe for the Clip property at 0:04 seconds where the title element is completely clipped, and an ending keyframe at 0:05 seconds where the title element is exposed. The resulting animation is a slow reveal, from left to right, of the yellow banner.

Animating shadows

Let's continue to add more sophisticated effects to your Edge Animate composition. The Shadow property displays different kinds of shadow effects for any of your elements, with options for the direction of the shadow, as well as the blurriness, color, and amount.

You'll add an animated shadow to the top banner, which will make the banner appear to separate from the background, and add a dramatic punch to highlight the show title.

Creating a drop shadow

A drop shadow has six components to it: color, position in the X direction, position in the Y direction, blur, spread, and whether it is a drop shadow or an inset shadow.

1 Move your playhead to the end of the animation at 0:05 seconds, and make sure that the Auto-Keyframe mode is off.

2 In the Properties panel, click on the Shadow toggle to enable the Shadow effect.

3 Click the color chip, and in the popup color picker, choose black (#000000) and change the A value (Alpha) to 60%.

The shadow is a slightly transparent black color.

4 Activate the Pin on the Timeline.

The Pin turns blue and Auto-Keyframe mode automatically turns on.

5 Drag the playhead to 0:05.500 seconds and keep the Pin at 0:05 seconds.

The playhead and the Pin separate. The starting point for the animation is set at 0:05 seconds and the ending point at 0:05.500 seconds.

6 Select the Clipping tool and drag the bottom edge of the bounding box downward. The value of the bottom Clip property should be 150 pixels.

You have to extend the clipping of your title element in order to accommodate the drop shadow, which extends past the bounds of the image.

● **Note:** Normally, you can create a drop shadow on an element without enlarging its Clip properties. However, in this composition, the element is currently being affected by clipping because of the animated reveal, so you have to take into account the current Clip boundaries.

● **Note:** Shadows can't be applied to groups, and shadows applied to symbol instances will be based on its rectangular bounding box.

7 In the Properties panel, change the Shadow properties to Y=25 pixels and the Blur to 14 pixels.

In the ending keyframes at 0:05.500 seconds, Edge Animate creates a soft shadow about 25 pixels thick that extends downward from the title element.

8 To complete this effect, change the horizontal and vertical Transform properties to 110% in the Properties panel.

The title banner enlarges slightly, in addition to the drop shadow that animates, drawing more attention to the graphic.

Working with advanced eases

While working with the final elements in this composition, you'll learn about the advanced options for easing. You'll display several fictional reviews for the television show. To keep things interesting, these last elements will sail onto the Stage and bounce into place. It'll take several bounces before the elements settle into their final resting positions, and you'll see how you can easily create that effect with the easing.

Importing the symbols

Earlier in this lesson, you learned to create and work with symbols. Now you'll import symbols that have already been created for you. The symbols are bundled in an Edge Animate Symbol file (with the extension .ansym).

1 Click the Plus button in the Symbols section of the Library panel and choose Import Symbols.

The Import Symbols from File dialog box appears.

2 Navigate to the 04Start folder and select the 04_symbols.ansym file and click Open.

Edge Animate imports three symbols and their associated image assets. You'll see review1, review2, and review3 appear in the Symbols folder of your Library panel.

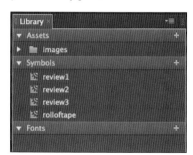

Adding the final elements

The review1, review2, and review3 symbols are the three fictional reviews.

1   Drag the review1, review2, and review3 symbols from the Library panel to the Stage.

2   Position review1 at X=312, Y=359. Position review2 at X=474, Y=462, and position review3 at X=739, Y=381.

3   In the Elements panel, arrange review3 at the top, review2 next, and review1 third from the top.

The reviews are in their final resting positions and ready to be animated.

Creating bouncing motion

You can create a bouncing effect to the motion of the reviews by applying the Bounce ease. The Bounce ease can be at the front of the motion, the end of the motion, or both the front and end. Bounces usually make sense only at the end (Ease Out), because, in real life, we're familiar with the bouncing effect of a ball coming to rest.

1   Activate the Pin on the Timeline.

The Pin turns blue and Auto-Keyframe mode automatically turns on.

2   Drag the playhead to 0:05.500 seconds and the Pin at 0:06.500 seconds.

The playhead and the Pin separate. The starting point for the animation is set at 0:05.500 seconds and the ending point at 0:06.500 seconds.

3 With the Selection tool, move each of the three reviews just off the Stage to the right.

Edge Animate creates beginning and ending keyframes for the Left properties for all the elements.

4 Select all three animation spans in the Timeline.

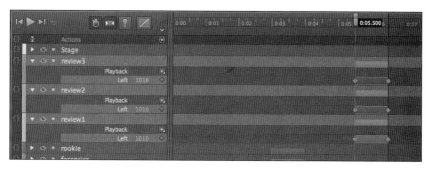

UNIVERSITY OF WINCHESTER
LIBRARY

5 At the top of the Timeline panel, click on the Easing button and choose Ease Out > Bounce.

Edge Animate applies the Bounce ease to the selected animated elements. The Bounce curve displays, in a graphical form, how the motion proceeds from the starting values to the ending values.

6 Turn off the Pin and preview your animation.

The review and tab elements ease out of their motion by bouncing. Each successive bounce is smaller, so the elements gradually end at their final positions.

Finishing touches

Your composition is complete! You've created a compelling animation that incorporates many of the more sophisticated techniques and effects that Edge Animate offers. Refine this project by playing around with the timing and pacing of each of the elements. Try and apply different eases to some of the other animations. For example, you can add an Ease In effect to the motion of the roll of tapes so they move more naturally.

You can open the 04End.html file in the Lesson04/04End folder again to view how your composition compares with the final project.

Review questions

1 How do you create Symbols, and what are they used for?

2 What is the difference between an instance and a symbol?

3 How do you create a looping animation inside a symbol?

4 What are Playback commands, and why are they useful?

5 What kind of effects can the Clipping tool make?

Review answers

1 You create a Symbol by selecting your elements and choosing Modify > Convert to Symbol, or by pressing Ctrl+Y (Windows) or Command+Y (Mac OS). Symbols are stored in the Library panel and are used to group together elements with an independent timeline. This allows the elements to have their own animation separate from the animation that is happening on the main Timeline panel.

2 An instance is a single element of the symbol definition in the Library panel. You can have multiple instances, which makes creating and editing complex animations simple. Each instance can be modified slightly on the main Stage, creating variations of the symbol.

3 You create a looping animation inside a symbol by adding a trigger on the symbol's timeline. A trigger is a simple command that tells Edge Animate to do something when the playhead reaches a certain point on the Timeline. Move the playhead to the end of the symbol's timeline, and choose Timeline > Insert Trigger, or press Ctrl+T (Windows) or Command+T (Mac OS). In the script pane that opens up, choose the Play from code snippet option, and enter 0 for the value in between the parentheses of the code.

4 Playback commands are options on the Timeline that change the initial behavior of your symbol instances. You can stop, play, play in reverse, or choose exact times to play your nested animation. You set the Playback options for *each* symbol instance, so individual instances of the same symbol can play their animations differently.

5 The Clipping tool controls how much of the element is visible. You can use the Clipping tool to crop the element's top, bottom, left, or right sides. You can animate the Clip values to achieve interesting cinematic effects, such as wipes.

5 ADDING BASIC INTERACTIVITY

Lesson overview

In this lesson, you'll learn how to do the following:

- Understand interactivity
- Work with the syntax of JavaScript
- Recognize the relationship between JavaScript, jQuery, and the Edge Animate API
- Differentiate triggers, events, and actions
- Add triggers to the Timeline
- Insert labels
- Create actions to respond to events
- Control the behavior of the Timeline playhead
- View and edit script with the Code panel
- Use comments to annotate code
- Hide and show elements to incorporate visual feedback for buttons
- Control animated elements
- Customize the mouse cursor

 This lesson will take approximately two hours to complete. If needed, remove the previous lesson folder from your hard drive and copy the Lesson05 folder onto it.

Let your viewers explore your composition and become active participants. Use Adobe Edge Animate's built-in code snippets and intuitive panels to add actions to create engaging, user-driven, interactive experiences.

Getting started

To begin, view the travel guide that you'll create as you learn to make interactive projects in Adobe Edge Animate.

1 Double-click the 05End.html file in the Lesson05/05End folder to play the composition in a browser.

The project is an interactive photo gallery showing images from Myanmar. Viewers can watch the short slideshow automatically play and loop back to the beginning. Or, viewers can click any thumbnail image on the left side of the Stage to go directly to a particular image. Move your mouse over the triangular button at the top to see a caption unravel.

In this lesson, you'll create interactive buttons with rollover highlights and learn to incorporate the proper code that tells Edge Animate where to move the playhead on the Timeline to display the particular animation or image there.

2 Close the 05End.html file and quit your browser.

3 Double-click the 05Start Edge Animate file in the Lesson05/05Start folder to open the initial project file in Edge Animate.

The file includes all the assets already placed on the Stage and the transitions between each image on the Timeline. The Stage has already been sized properly. In this lesson, you'll make this linear animation interactive.

4 Choose File > Save As. Name the file **05_workingcopy** and save it in the 05Start folder. Saving a working copy ensures that the original start file will be available if you want to start over.

About interactive compositions

Interactive compositions change based on the viewer's actions. For example, when the viewer clicks a button, a different graphic with more information could appear. Interactivity can be simple, such as the click of a button, or it can be more complex, involving different kinds of interactions with the same element—for example, moving your mouse cursor over a button, clicking the button, and moving your mouse cursor off the button are three unique events that could each result in different visual changes on the Stage.

In Edge Animate, you use JavaScript to achieve interactivity. JavaScript is a popular and standard script for Web browsers. JavaScript runs on browsers for desktops as well as on devices such as tablets and mobile phones.

If you have no idea what JavaScript is, or how to write code—don't panic! Adobe Edge Animate provides an easy interface to add JavaScript to your compositions and integrate common interactive functions. When you get more comfortable with the syntax of the script, you can begin to delve deeper and customize the interactivity.

In this lesson, you'll learn to create nonlinear navigation, meaning the animation doesn't have to play straight from the beginning to the end, and stop there. You'll add code that gets triggered when the playhead reaches a certain point in time. You'll also add code that moves the playhead to different parts of the Timeline to display particular elements. You'll also learn to make elements on the Stage respond to different interactions with the mouse cursor.

Understanding JavaScript

JavaScript is the scripting language that adds additional functionality to a Web page. Many of the common interface elements on websites, such as pull-down menus, check boxes, or search boxes, are created with JavaScript. Edge Animate also uses JavaScript to power its interactivity, as well as the animations and other effects.

Where the JavaScript lives

Even without adding any interactivity to your composition, your project depends on JavaScript. The JavaScript code is contained in several separate text documents that have the file extension ".js". Look at the files associated with your Edge Animate composition, 05_workingcopy. There are four JavaScript files within the folder called edge_includes:

- edge.1.0.0.min.js

- jquery-1.7.1.min.js

- jquery.easing.1.3.js

- json2_min.js

These files contain the basic code required for any Edge Animate composition. There are also additional JavaScript files, which are unique to your project. Those files are located outside the edge_includes folder, and are automatically named with your Edge Animate filename. Your files are named as follows:

- 05_workingcopy_edge.js

- 05_workingcopy_edgeActions.js

- 05_workingcopy_edgePreload.js

When your Web browser first launches your Edge Animate project, it loads the JavaScript code so all the functionality is available when your project plays. All the code is organized as functions, which group commands together. Since each function has a unique name, you can trigger the commands simply by referencing the name of the function. Programmers say that a function is "called," or that the browser "calls" a function.

jQuery and the Edge Animate API

While JavaScript is useful, it's meant to control all the details of a Web page, which is powerful but often clumsy and complicated. That's where jQuery and the Edge Animate API come in handy. jQuery is an open-source JavaScript library that provides an easy way to select, control, and animate elements in a browser. jQuery is not another language, but simply a set of well-written JavaScript functions. If you look again at the JavaScript files in the edge_includes folder, you'll see that two of those files are, in fact, files for jQuery.

Along with jQuery, Edge Animate provides additional functions it has built for you. The library of JavaScript functions that Edge Animate has built for your use constitute the Edge Animate API (Application Programming Interface).

You can think of JavaScript, jQuery, and the Edge Animate API as different layers of control. The Edge Animate API is the top, most superficial layer of control, jQuery is the middle, and the core JavaScript is the deepest layer. A useful analogy is the control of an automobile. The Edge Animate API would represent the controls you see in the driver's seat—the steering wheel, the parking brake, or the gas pedal. They allow you to drive the car without needing to know much about its inner workings. They're created from a combination of levers, dials, and shafts to make controlling your vehicle simple and easy. Those levers, dials, and shafts represent the jQuery level of control. At the most granular level, you have JavaScript, represented by the individual nuts and bolts and gears.

Just as it is so much easier to drive a car using the steering wheel and gas pedal, so it is to control your Edge Animate composition with the Edge Animate API. But in both cases, there's no reason why you couldn't tinker with the deeper-level controls for a more customized experience. You can start coding in jQuery and JavaScript to make your own interactivity. You just need to be sure you're a competent mechanic, or know your way around JavaScript!

In this lesson, you'll first learn to add interactivity with the Edge Animate API. Later, as you gain more confidence and comfort, you'll delve a little deeper and insert some jQuery for more sophisticated effects.

Triggers, events, and actions

Edge Animate uses actions, triggers, and events to incorporate JavaScript in your composition.

Actions are the things that Edge Animate can do, which, given the full JavaScript language at its disposal, is quite a lot. Actions can range from loading a hyperlink, to changing a particular visual property of an element on the Stage, to storing a piece of information in a variable for later retrieval.

Triggers are actions that are placed along the Timeline. When the playhead reaches the trigger, the actions are executed. Use triggers when you want code to be synchronized by your animation, and not by user control.

Events are things that happen in a composition that Edge Animate can respond to with an action. Typically, events are user-generated, such as the click of a mouse button, the pressing down of a key, or the tilting of a mobile device. However, events can also happen automatically. For example, the point when the composition is ready (when all the assets and code libraries have been downloaded) is an event. Events are always paired with actions. When an event happens, an action— or set of actions—is executed.

Timeline triggers

Triggers are the simplest way to add code to your Edge Animate composition. Triggers are executed automatically when the playhead reaches them on the Timeline. You can have multiple triggers along the Timeline. The minimum time interval between triggers is 1/1000th of a second, but practically, you'd never need or want actions to be executed so close together.

Creating a loop

For this slideshow of Myanmar, you'll insert a trigger at the end of the Timeline to make the playhead automatically return to the beginning, creating a loop.

1 Click the Zoom Timeline to Fit button at the bottom of the Timeline.

The entire slideshow animation appears in the available space in the Timeline panel.

2 Move the playhead to the very end of the slideshow, at 0:10 seconds.

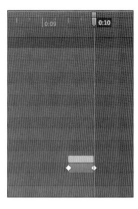

3 In the Timeline panel, click the Insert Trigger button on the top Actions row. You can also choose Timeline > Insert Trigger or press Ctrl+T (Windows) or Command+T (Mac OS).

An icon that appears as a diamond enclosed by curly braces appears on the Timeline at 0:10 seconds. The icon represents a trigger.

A panel appears with a large white text-entry field and a column of code snippet options on the right side. The panel is titled Trigger@10000ms, referring to the trigger's position at 10,000 milliseconds, or 10 seconds.

4 View the content of the current script.

The current script, //insert code here, is known as a comment. Comments always begin with two backslash characters, and are descriptions of the code. Comments are non-functional, and don't significantly add to the file size of your composition.

5 From the menu of code snippets on the right-hand side of the panel, select the Play from option.

New code appears in the panel after the existing comment. The new code comes with its own comments that describe its function. The code, sym.play(1000);, moves the playhead to a particular point in time on the Timeline and begins playing.

● **Note:** The number in between the parentheses of the play() command is called the *argument*. It gives the command additional information to make it more specific. In this case, it tells the command at what millisecond point in time to start playing. Commands can have multiple arguments, which are separated by commas. As you learn more commands, you also learn what arguments they require.

6 Replace the 1000 within the parentheses in the code with **0**.

The number in between the parentheses of the play() command represents the time to which the playhead will move. Since you want the playhead to move to the beginning of the Timeline at 0:00 seconds, enter **0** in the parentheses of the play() command.

7 Close the panel and preview your project in a browser by pressing Ctrl+Enter (Windows) or Command+Return (Mac OS).

The slideshow plays through and repeats when it reaches the end at 10 seconds.

Editing triggers

Editing the script for your triggers is simple and easy. The panel that appeared when you added the trigger is always available for modifications, additions, or deletions.

- **To edit a trigger**, double-click the trigger icon on the Timeline.

  The script panel opens to display the trigger, and you can modify the argument, delete the code, or add new code from the snippet options on the right side of the panel.

- **To move a trigger**, click and drag the trigger icon on the Timeline to a new position.

  The trigger moves to a different position, so the actions are executed when the playhead reaches a new time.

- **To delete a trigger**, select the trigger on the Timeline and press the Delete key.

  The trigger is removed from the Timeline.

Script panel viewing options

The script panel that opens when you add a trigger has several options to help you make viewing the code easier. The top-right options menu has three choices that control what's displayed.

- **Show Line Numbers** displays sequential numbers next to each line of code so you and other developers who share the script can pinpoint code.

- **Font Size** controls the display size (Small, Medium, or Large) of the text in the script. The default option is Small.

- **Include Snippet Comments** automatically adds comments to the code that you add from the snippet options on the right side of the panel.

In addition to these display options, you can click the vertical border that divides the white script area with the menu of code snippets to collapse the menu to make more room for your code. Click the divider again to expand the menu.

Minding your syntax

Let's examine the code that you added in the trigger more closely to learn about JavaScript *syntax*, or the way words and punctuation work together. Syntax is the grammar of a programming language.

If you're unfamiliar with program code or scripting, the JavaScript code that Edge Animate inserts may be challenging to decipher. However, once you understand the basic syntax, you'll find it easier to follow a script.

The code that is in your trigger at 10000 milliseconds appears as follows:

```
sym.play(0);
```

- The first word in the statement is `sym`. When the statement is on the main Timeline, the word `sym` represents the whole Edge Animate composition. Edge Animate is organized around the concept of "symbols," and the root, or base-level symbol, is the Edge Animate Stage. This root symbol contains all the elements and animations in your Edge Animate composition—everything on the Stage or Timeline. In JavaScript, when we want to do something, you first identify the object that you want to control. In this case, since you want to affect the Timeline of your Edge Animate composition, the first thing that is written in the script is `sym`.

- The *dot* operator (`.`) provides a way to access different commands for the object that you've identified (in this case, `sym`). Objects can be animations, text, or abstract concepts such as the date or particular data. Objects have *properties*, which describe them, and *methods*, which are the things that they can do. In your trigger, the method for the `sym` object is `play()`. The dot, or period, separates the object and its method.

- As in English, every open *parenthesis* must have a corresponding close parenthesis, and the same is true for JavaScript. If you open something, you must close it. All methods have parentheses. You method, `play()`, has an open and close parenthesis.

- Each method can have different *arguments* in between the parentheses, which provide additional information. The `play()` method requires a single argument, which tells Edge Animate at what point in time (in milliseconds) to begin playing. Methods can have multiple arguments, which are separated by commas.

- Some arguments require a number, some may need a name, and others may need the words `true` or `false`. Whenever you're entering the name of a file or a URL, use *single or double quotation marks*. Quotation marks distinguish a *String* value, which represent a sequence of characters, with other kinds of values.

- You can add *comments* to remind you or others of what you are accomplishing with different parts of the script. To add a comment for a single line, start it with two slashes (//). To type a multiline comment, start it with /* and end it with */. Comments are ignored by JavaScript and won't affect your code at all.

- The *semicolon* at the end of the line tells JavaScript that it has reached the end of a complete statement and the end of a line of code. A semicolon is like a period in a sentence.

That's a lot of information packed into a single line of code! But getting comfortable with the syntax is your first step in getting out from behind the steering wheel and looking under the hood of your car.

Events and actions

So far, you've seen how Edge Animate uses triggers to automatically execute JavaScript when the playhead reaches a certain point on the Timeline. You added a trigger at the end of the animation to create a loop. The other two ways with which Edge Animate adds JavaScript is with events and actions.

Events are occurrences that happen in Edge Animate that it can detect and respond to. When an event is detected, you provide *actions* as a response.

It's useful to think of interactions in terms of events and actions. When you click on a menu button (event), more options may expand (actions). When you roll over a button (event), a triangular play icon may appear on it (actions). In the next section, you'll add thumbnail images to the Stage. When the user clicks on each thumbnail (event), the playhead will move to a new position on the Timeline (actions) to show a particular image from the travel slideshow.

Creating the buttons

A button is a basic visual indicator of what the user can interact with. The user usually clicks a button, but many other types of interactions are possible. For example, rollovers, double-clicks, and rollouts are all possible. Edge Animate also provides events unique to mobile devices, such as touches.

You'll start with the simplest, and most common event, which is the single-click.

Adding the thumbnails

Small, cropped versions of the larger Myanmar images are provided for you in the images folder.

1 In the Library panel, expand the images folder within the Assets folder.

2 Drag the file called button1_gray.jpg from the Library panel to the Stage.

A grayscale thumbnail of a fisherman appears on the Stage, Timeline, and Elements panel.

3 Position the thumbnail so that its top-left corner is at the top-left corner of the Stage. The coordinates should be at X=0, Y=0.

4 Drag the file called button2_gray.jpg from the Library panel to the Stage, and position it just below the first thumbnail. You can use the smart guides to help automatically snap the images in place. The coordinates should be at X=0, Y=80.

Two grayscale thumbnails are at the left side of the Stage, one above the other.

5 Drag the remaining three grayscale thumbnails from the Library panel onto the Stage, positioning each successive one below the previous one.

There should be a total of five thumbnail images vertically stacked on the left side of the Stage.

Adding the events

Each element on the Stage can have its own events and actions. Insert code for individual elements from the far-left column of the Timeline or Elements panel. The Open Actions button is indicated by a set of curly braces.

1 In the Timeline or the Elements panel, click the Open Actions button for the first thumbnail element, button1_gray.

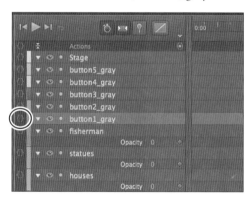 

The script panel for button1_gray opens.

A menu of options automatically opens, displaying the events that are possible for the button1_gray element.

Note: As you add more events to the same element, additional tabs appear at the top of the script panel.

2 Select the first option: click.

Edge Animate adds a click tab at the top of the panel with an empty script pane and available snippets on the right.

Note: To delete an event (and any code associated with it), select the particular tab for the event and click the Minus button at the top-left corner of the script panel.

Adding the actions

Each event must have an accompanying action, or a response, to the event.

1 Position your cursor on the second line of the script pane (after the first line of comments), and choose the Stop at option.

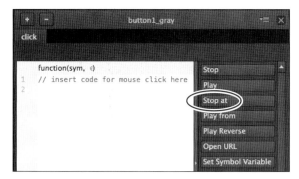

Edge Animate adds the code to stop the playhead at a particular position on the Timeline.

2 In between the parentheses of the stop() method, replace the 1000 number with **0**.

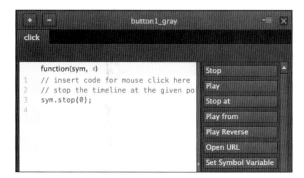

The stop() method requires a number, in milliseconds, of the point on the Timeline at which it will move to and stop. Since this first grayscale thumbnail is of the fisherman, you want the playhead to stop at 0:00 seconds, the point at which we see the full image of the fishermen on the Stage.

● **Note:** You can actually use any number between 0 and 1500 for the stop() method for button1_gray, since the image of the fishermen remains on the Timeline until 1.5 seconds, but it's simpler and easier to be consistent to pick the time when the image first appears.

3   Close the script panel.

The Open Actions icon for the button1_gray element becomes filled in, indicating that there is currently script attached to that element.

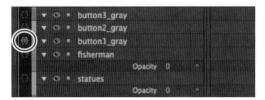

4   Preview your Edge Animate composition in a browser by selecting File > Preview in browser, or pressing Ctrl+Enter (Windows)/Command+Return (Mac OS).

5   At any point during the slideshow, click the first grayscale thumbnail.

The slideshow stops and shows the image of the fishermen.

Completing the interactivity

Now that you've completed the interactivity for the first button, add the same functionality to the remainder.

1   In the Timeline or the Elements panel, click the Open Actions button for the second thumbnail element, button2_gray.

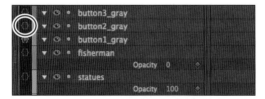

The script panel for button2_gray opens.

2   Click on the Plus button on the upper-left corner.

A menu of options opens, displaying the events that are possible for the button2_gray element.

3 Select the first option: click.

Edge Animate adds a click tab at the top of the panel with an empty script pane and available snippets on the right.

4 Position your cursor on the second line of the script pane (after the first line of comments), and choose the Stop at option.

Edge Animate adds the JavaScript code to stop the playhead at a particular position on the Timeline.

5 In between the parentheses of the stop() method, replace the 1000 number with **2000**.

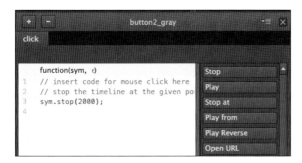

The stop() method requires a number, in milliseconds, of the point on the Timeline at which it will move to and stop. Since the second grayscale thumbnail is of the statues, you want the playhead to stop at 0:02 seconds, the point at which we see the full image of the statues on the Stage.

6 Add similar click events to all the other grayscale thumbnail images, with the Stop at option. Be sure to change the arguments for each stop() method as follows, so the playhead stops at different times to display a unique larger image on the Stage:

- The stop() method for button1_gray should go to 0 milliseconds.
- The stop() method for button2_gray should go to 2000 milliseconds.
- The stop() method for button3_gray should go to 4000 milliseconds.
- The stop() method for button4_gray should go to 6000 milliseconds.
- The stop() method for button5_gray should go to 8000 milliseconds.

Navigating the Code panel

Your travel slideshow is now interactive, where users can click to see any of the images. But your code appears to be scattered among many different elements. How can you view all the code for your Edge Animate composition together? The answer is in the Code panel, which you can open by choosing Window > Code, or pressing Ctrl+E (Windows) or Command+E (Mac OS).

Viewing your code

The Code panel displays all the code in your Edge Animate composition—both the code that is automatically generated for every project, and the code that you insert yourself.

1 Choose Window > Code, or press Ctrl+E (Windows)/Command+E (Mac OS).

The Code panel opens. The Code panel is similar to the other script panels for triggers, events, and actions.

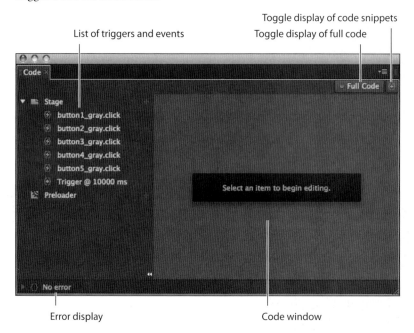

List of triggers and events

Toggle display of code snippets

Toggle display of full code

Error display

Code window

2 Click on the Full Code button on the far-right side of the panel to toggle
between Full Code mode and non-Full Code mode.

In Full Code mode, Edge Animate displays the entire code for the JavaScript
file for the Edge Animate composition. Scroll down to see the script for all
your thumbnail elements as well as the trigger. The code that this represents is
contained in the file 05_workingcopy_edgeActions.js.

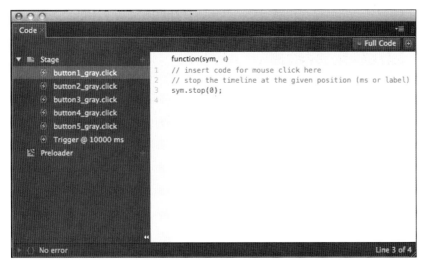

In non-Full Code mode, you can select the code for the individual elements
or triggers on the Stage on the left side of the panel. In addition, there is an
option to see the code for the Preloader, which is currently disabled because you
haven't yet added one. In later lessons, you'll learn about adding a Preloader.

3 While in non-Full Code mode, click on the Plus button in line with the Stage element.

A hierarchical menu appears that allows you to add an event to the Stage itself, an event to any of the elements on the Stage, or an event to the Timeline.

4 If you want to delete an event or trigger from the Code panel, right-click on the event or trigger from the list and select Delete Action.

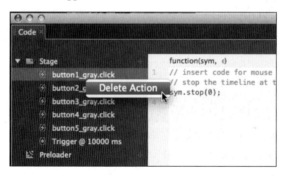

5 In either Full Code or non-Full Code mode, when you make additions and edits to the script, and they are saved in the composition.

Dealing with code errors

Using the provided code snippets makes adding code relatively easy because the script is already formatted correctly. All you have to do is replace key values. However, bugs and typos do invariably creep in, and dealing with code errors is a common struggle for any developer, whether a novice or an expert.

Edge Animate immediately alerts you to code errors, which make finding and correcting them easy. When there is a mistake in syntax in any of the code, Edge Animate displays an error message at the bottom-left corner of the Code panel. For example, if you were to accidentally delete the closing parenthesis of the stop() method, the error display tells you where the error occurs. In addition, a red dot appears next to the line of code in question.

The error notification is also displayed at the bottom-left corner of the Stage.

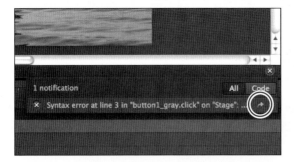

Click on the arrow icon after the error description to jump directly to the source of the error in the Code panel so you can fix it. The All or Code options in the error display determines whether all errors are displayed (including warnings of feature incompatibilities with various devices, such as text shadows in IE9), or only code errors are displayed.

Creating labels

When the user clicks each thumbnail, Edge Animate moves the playhead to a new time on the Timeline, according to the argument in the stop() method. However, imagine that the client who has commissioned you to develop this slideshow wants the whole sequence to run a little slower. That's an easy task to do because you can select all of the elements on the Timeline and move all the keyframes and animations forward to lengthen the total amount of time. But doing so causes the times that each image appears on the Stage to change, which would require you to change all the millisecond values in the stop() methods.

There is an alternate approach that would save you time and effort. Instead of using fixed-millisecond times in the stop() methods, you can use labels, which refer to points on the Timeline. Labels can move with your animation, so increasing or decreasing the length of your animation can move the labels proportionately.

Adding labels

Labels appear on the Timeline panel, below the time markers and just above the Actions layer.

1 Move the playhead to 0:00 seconds.

The image of the fishermen appears at 0:00 seconds.

2 Click the Insert Label button, or press Ctrl+L (Windows)/Command+L (Mac OS).

A label appears on the Timeline, named Label 1.

3 Rename the label **fisherman**, and press Enter to exit the text editing of the label.

The label called fisherman is now associated with 0:00 seconds.

4 Add four more labels to the Timeline, each marking the starting point at which an image appears on the Stage.

- Insert the label **statues** at 0:02 seconds.

- Insert the label **houses** at 0:04 seconds.

- Insert the label **monk** at 0:06 seconds.

- Insert the label **women** at 0:08 seconds.

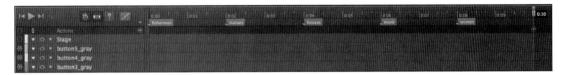

Editing labels

There are several ways you can edit labels once you've inserted and named them:

- **To rename a label**, double-click the label name on the Timeline.

- **To move a label**, click and drag the label on the Timeline to a new position.

- **To delete a label**, select the label on the Timeline so it is highlighted and press the Delete key.

- **To cut, copy, or paste a label**, right-click on a label and choose your desired option, or use the standard keyboard commands for cut (Ctrl/Command+X), copy (Ctrl/Command+C), and paste (Ctrl/Command+V).

Changing the references to the Timeline

Now that the Timeline contains labels, you can change the references in the JavaScript code.

1 Choose Window > Code, or press Ctrl+E (Windows)/Command+E (Mac OS).

  The Code panel opens.

2 If it is not already selected, click the Full Code button to display the panel in Full Code mode.

  All the code for the thumbnail events and actions are displayed in the single script pane.

```
                                                                              ● Full Code
65
66      Symbol.bindElementAction(compId, symbolName, "${_button1_gray}", "click", function(sym, e) {
67          // insert code for mouse click here
68          // stop the timeline at the given position (ms or label)
69          sym.stop(0);
70
71      });
72      //Edge binding end
73
74      Symbol.bindElementAction(compId, symbolName, "${_button2_gray}", "click", function(sym, e) {
75          // insert code for mouse click here
76          // stop the timeline at the given position (ms or label)
77          sym.stop(2000);
78
79      });
80      //Edge binding end
81
82      Symbol.bindElementAction(compId, symbolName, "${_button3_gray}", "click", function(sym, e) {
83          // stop the timeline at the given position (ms or label)
84          sym.stop(4000);
85          // insert code for mouse click here
86
87      });
88      //Edge binding end
89
90      Symbol.bindElementAction(compId, symbolName, "${_button4_gray}", "click", function(sym, e) {
91          // insert code for mouse click here
92          // stop the timeline at the given position (ms or label)
93          sym.stop(6000);
94
95      });
96      //Edge binding end
97
98      Symbol.bindElementAction(compId, symbolName, "${_button5_gray}", "click", function(sym, e) {
99          // insert code for mouse click here
100         // stop the timeline at the given position (ms or label)
101         sym.stop(8000);
102
103     });
104     //Edge binding end
105
```

● Note: Make sure that you are using straight quotation marks around your label names. The quotation marks are essential for JavaScript to identify the names as a String (and not a variable). Straight quotes and curly quotes (or smart quotes) are different characters in HTML and JavaScript and they are not interchangeable.

3 Replace all the millisecond times in the `stop()` methods with your labels. The following lines of code should be changed:

- Change `sym.stop(0);` to `sym.stop("fisherman");`

- Change `sym.stop(2000);` to `sym.stop("statues");`

- Change `sym.stop(4000);` to `sym.stop("houses");`

- Change `sym.stop(6000);` to `sym.stop("monk");`

- Change `sym.stop(8000);` to `sym.stop("women");`

4 Preview your Edge Animate composition in a browser by choosing File > Preview in the browser, or pressing Ctrl+Enter (Windows)/Command+Return (Mac OS).

5 At any point during the slideshow, click the thumbnail images.

The slideshow stops and shows the selected image.

6 Return to Edge Animate and select all the elements on the Timeline by choosing Select > All, or by pressing Ctrl+A (Windows)/Command+A (Mac OS). Make sure none of the elements are locked.

7 Click and drag the last keyframe of the last animated element on the Timeline. Drag the keyframe to the left to decrease the total amount of time of the slideshow.

As you decrease the length of time for all the animated elements, the labels also move proportionally, preserving their identification of what's displayed on the Stage. Return the total time of the composition to 0:10 seconds.

Adding visual feedback

Most interactive elements on the Web feature visual feedback, which is important to provide clues to the reader that the particular item is interactive. For example, a simple hyperlink on a Web page often will change color when you move your mouse over it. A button will highlight when you move your mouse over it, and may appear depressed when you click on it.

You can create these interactions with a combination of events and actions in Edge Animate. You'll add these events and actions to the thumbnails for visual feedback next.

Adding the mouseover thumbnails

The first question you should ask is, what visual effect do you want to see when a user moves their mouse over the thumbnail images? For this project, you'll make the grayscale thumbnails become colorized and a highlight appear around the borders. The first step is to bring colorized versions of the thumbnails on to the Stage.

1 In the images folder in the Assets folder of the Library panel, you'll find color versions of each of the five thumbnail images, indicated by the _color appended to the file name.

2 Drag button1_color.jpg from the Library on to the Stage.

3 Use the Smart Guides to position the button1_color element at the upper-left corner, exactly on top of its grayscale version. Its location should be at X=0, Y=0.

4 Drag all four of the other colorized versions of the thumbnails to the Stage, positioning them exactly on top of their grayscale partners. All the colored thumbnails should be at the top of the Element panel stack.

The grayscale and colorized versions of the thumbnails are exactly the same dimensions.

Hiding the mouseover thumbnails

Since you want to show the colorized version only when the mouse cursor moves over the thumbnail, you must first hide the colorized thumbnails. You can hide the elements by changing their Display property to Off.

1 Move the playhead to 0:00 seconds.

2 Hold down the Shift key and select all the colorized thumbnail elements.

3 In the Properties panel, change the Display property from Always On to Off.

Edge Animate inserts a new keyframe on the Timeline for all the selected elements at 0:00 seconds and the selected elements disappear from the Stage.

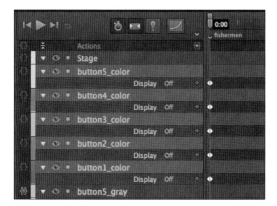

Inserting the mouseover event

Each grayscale thumbnail contains a click event. You'll have to edit each of those elements to incorporate a mouseover event. A *mouseover event* happens when the user moves their mouse cursor over the selected element. When the mouseover event happens, you'll show the colorized thumbnails.

1 In the Timeline or the Elements panel, click the Open Actions button for the first thumbnail element, button1_gray.

The script panel for button1_gray opens. The current click event and actions appear.

2 Click on the Plus button on the upper-left corner and choose mouseover.

Edge Animate adds a mouseover tab.

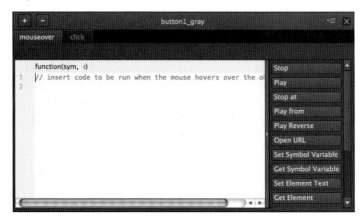

3 Position your cursor on the second line of the script pane (after the first line of comments), and choose the Show Element option.

Edge Animate adds the JavaScript code to display an element. The highlighted portion of the code is the name of the element to display.

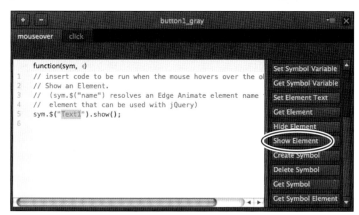

4 Replace the highlighted code with **button1_color**. Make sure that the double straight quotation marks remain around your element name.

The full statement appears as follows:

```
sym.$("button1_color").show();
```

The dollar sign and parentheses is jQuery syntax, and it tells the browser what element to select. In this statement, the element called button1_color in the current Edge Animate composition is selected, and the method called show() is executed.

5 Preview your Edge Animate composition in a browser by choosing File > Preview in your browser or pressing Ctrl+Enter (Windows)/Command+Return (Mac OS). Move your mouse over the first grayscale thumbnail image.

As soon as your mouse cursor moves over the grayscale thumbnail image, the colorized version appears. Since the colorized version is above the grayscale version, we see only the colorized image.

6 Return to Edge Animate and insert the mouseover event with the Show Element action to the remaining four grayscale thumbnail buttons. Make sure to replace the highlighted code portion with the correct colorized version of the thumbnail.

Inserting the mouseout event

When you preview the Edge Animate project, you'll notice that the thumbnails become colorized when you move your mouse over them, but they remain in color even after you move your mouse off them. In order to make the thumbnails revert to their grayscale versions, you need to add one additional event: the mouseout event.

The *mouseout* event happens when the cursor moves off an element. You'll add the mouseout event to the *colorized* thumbnails (not the grayscale thumbnails) and pair the event with a command that hides the colorized versions. The result: The colorized versions disappear, leaving the grayscale version visible again.

1 In the Timeline or the Elements panel, click the Open Actions button for the thumbnail element button1_color. The element is currently hidden on the Stage, but you can still add script to it.

The script panel for button1_color opens.

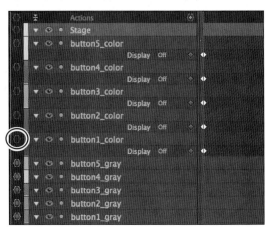

2 In the popup menu that appears, choose mouseout for the event.

Edge Animate adds a mouseout tab.

3 Position your cursor on the second line of the script pane (after the first line of comments), and choose the Hide Element option.

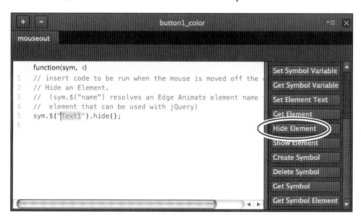

Edge Animate adds the JavaScript code to display an element. The highlighted portion of the code is the name of the element to display.

4 Replace the highlighted code with **button1_color**. Make sure that the double straight quotation marks remain around your element name.

The full statement appears as follows:

```
sym.$("button1_color").hide();
```

Note the similarities between the actions for this mouseout event and the previous script for the mouseover event.

5   Preview your Edge Animate composition in a browser by choosing File > Preview in your browser or pressing Ctrl+Enter (Windows)/Command+Return (Mac OS). Move your mouse over the first grayscale thumbnail image.

As soon as your mouse cursor moves over the grayscale thumbnail image, it becomes colorized. When you move your mouse cursor off the image, the button appears to revert back to grayscale.

6   Return to Edge Animate and insert the mouseout event with the Hide Element action to the remaining four colorized thumbnail buttons. Make sure to replace the highlighted code portion with the correct colorized version of the thumbnail.

Editing the click event

One final fix is needed before all the events and actions work together. You may have noticed that clicking on the buttons doesn't move the playhead as you intend. The reason it no longer works is because the colorized thumbnails overlap their grayscale counterparts, which block the click events. Your final step is to remove the click event from the grayscale thumbnails and add them to the colorized thumbnails instead.

1   In the Timeline or the Elements panel, click the Open Actions button for each of the grayscale thumbnail elements.

2   Choose the click event tab on the script panel, and click the Minus button.

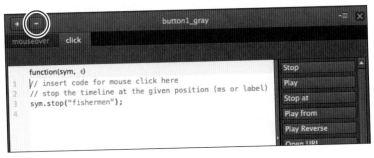

Edge Animate deletes the click event and all of its actions.

3   In the Timeline or the Elements panel, click the Open Actions button for each of the colorized thumbnail elements.

4 Click on the Plus button on the upper-left corner and choose click for the event.

Edge Animate adds a click event tab.

5 Choose the Stop at option, and as you did before, replace the millisecond argument with the corresponding label on the Timeline.

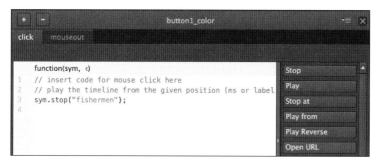

6 Preview your Edge Animate composition in a browser by choosing File > Preview in your browser or pressing Ctrl+Enter (Windows)/Command+Return (Mac OS).

Your buttons are complete. When you move your mouse over them, they become colorized. When you move your mouse off them, they revert to grayscale, and when you click on them, Edge Animate displays the corresponding image from the slideshow.

● **Note:** Use the Code panel and choose the Full Code mode to make global edits to your script easier. You can save time and effort if you're careful about selecting and editing code.

Customizing the mouse cursor

In addition to the visual feedback that you can provide by changing the appearance of the button when the user interacts with it, you can also change the appearance of the cursor itself. Often, the default arrow cursor on a desktop or laptop browser changes to a hand (known as the *pointer* cursor) when it hovers over an interactive element or hyperlink. You can choose to change the cursor to a pointer, or choose from among dozens of other cursor types.

Using the pointer

The Properties panel controls the cursor appearance and allows you to select a custom icon for each element.

1 In the Timeline panel, temporarily turn the Display property for the five colorized thumbnail elements to On.

Turning on the Display property allows you to select them on the Stage.

2 Select all five colorized thumbnail elements, button1_color through button5_color.

3 In the Properties panel, click the Cursor option and choose the pointer icon.

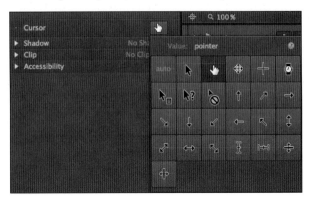

4 Turn the Display property for the five colorized thumbnail elements back to Off.

The colorized thumbnail elements are hidden again.

5 Preview your Edge Animate composition in a browser by choosing File > Preview in your browser or pressing Ctrl+Enter (Windows)/Command+Return (Mac OS).

The pointer cursor appears whenever you move your mouse over or click on the buttons.

● **Note:** You can only change the appearance of the cursor for each element, and not for every event of an element.

Controlling animated elements

So far, you've added JavaScript that controlled the behavior of the playhead and the hiding or displaying of particular elements. You can also add code to control the playback of animated symbols.

Symbols, as you learned in the previous lesson, are independent objects that you create that can have their own internal animation. With JavaScript, you can control the symbol animations to create more sophisticated interactions. For example, you can create a button that controls a dramatic animated unfurling or closing of a map. Or, you can create a button that controls the animated expansion or collapse of a more info box. The map and the more info box would be symbols that behave independently on the main Timeline.

For your interactive travel slideshow, you'll add a button at the top of the Stage that, when rolled over, elegantly animates to reveal information about the images and Myanmar.

Adding the button and animated symbol

The button and the animated symbol have already been created for you, and are in the Library ready to use.

1   In the Library panel, expand the Symbols section, and drag the moreinfo symbol to the Stage. Position the moreinfo symbol at X=200, Y=0.

The moreinfo symbol appears in the Elements and Timeline panels. The short playback arrowheads on the Timeline show how long the animation within the symbol lasts (1 second long).

2 In the Timeline, click the Playback options for the moreinfo element and choose Stop.

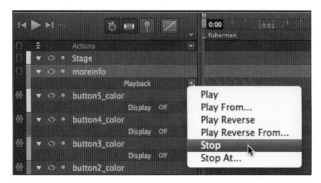

The playback of the internal symbol animation does not play on the main Timeline.

3 Double-click the moreinfo symbol on the Stage and press the spacebar to view the animation within the symbol.

The symbol consists of two short animations. The long horizontal gray rectangle expands, and at the same time, the clipping box of some informational text expands to reveal it.

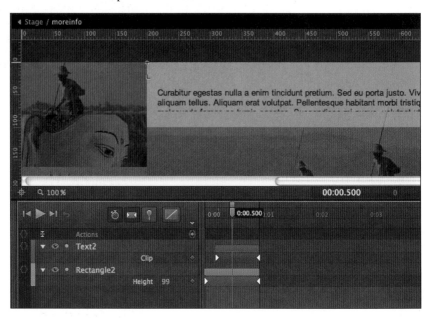

4 Click the Stage button at the top of the Stage to exit your symbol.

5 Drag the triangle.png image from the Library Assets folder to the Stage. Position the triangle element at X=484, Y=3, or use the Smart Guides to center the element over the moreinfo element.

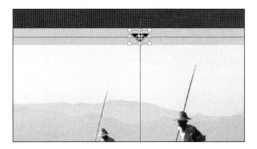

Play a symbol animation

The symbol is currently stopped at 0 seconds. You'll add a mouseover event to the triangle button that tells the symbol to begin playing.

1 In the Timeline or the Elements panel, click the Open Actions button for the triangle element.

The script panel for triangle opens.

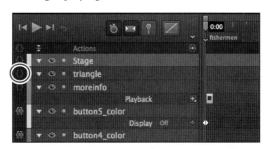

2 Choose mouseover for the event.

Edge Animate adds a mouseover event tab.

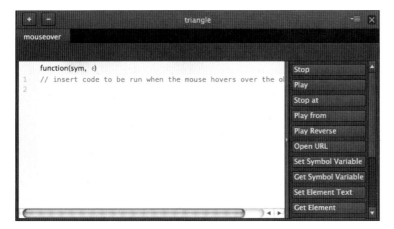

3 Choose the Get Symbol option.

Edge Animate adds the JavaScript code to select a particular symbol on the Stage. The highlighted portion of the code is the name of the symbol that you want to select.

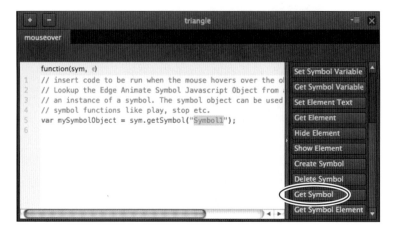

4 Replace the highlighted code with **moreinfo**, to match the moreinfo element on the Stage. Make sure that the double straight quotation marks remain around your element name.

The full statement appears as follows:

```
var mySymbolObject = sym.getSymbol("moreinfo");
```

The first part of this statement, `var mySymbolObject`, creates a variable for the reference to your symbol, so you can control it.

```
function(sym, e)
1    // insert code to be run when the mouse hovers over the o
2    // Lookup the Edge Animate Symbol Javascript Object from
3    // an instance of a symbol. The symbol object can be used
4    // symbol functions like play, stop etc.
5    var mySymbolObject = sym.getSymbol("moreinfo");
6
```

5 On the next line in the script panel, choose the Play option.

Edge Animate adds a statement that plays the `sym` object, or the main Timeline. However, you want the symbol to play its animation, not the animation on the main Timeline.

6   Replace `sym` with the variable, `mySymbolObject`, which refers to your symbol.

```
function(sym, e)
1    // insert code to be run when the mouse hovers over the ol
2    // Lookup the Edge Animate Symbol Javascript Object from
3    // an instance of a symbol. The symbol object can be used
4    // symbol functions like play, stop etc.
5    var mySymbolObject = sym.getSymbol("moreinfo");
6    mySymbolObject.play();
7
```

The next statement appears as follows:

```
mySymbolObject.play();
```

Note: You can combine the two statements into one line as follows:
`sym.getSymbol("moreinfo").play();`

Reset the symbol animation

Now, you'll add a mouseout event for the triangle element to move its playhead
back to 0 seconds to reset the animation.

1   In the Timeline or the Elements panel, click the Open Actions button for the
    triangle element.

    The script panel for moreinfo button opens.

2   Click on the Plus button
    on the upper-left corner
    and choose mouseout
    for the event.

    Edge Animate adds a
    mouseout event tab.

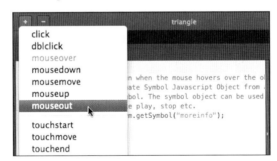

3   Choose the Get Symbol option, and replace the highlighted code
    with **moreinfo**.

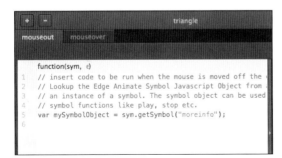

The full statement appears as follows:

```
var mySymbolObject = sym.getSymbol("moreinfo");
```

4 On the next line in the script panel, choose the Stop at option.

Edge Animate adds a statement that stops the sym object, or the main Timeline. However, you want the symbol to stop its animation, not the animation on the main Timeline.

5 Replace sym with the variable, mySymbolObject, which refers to your symbol. Replace the 1000 default millisecond argument with **0**.

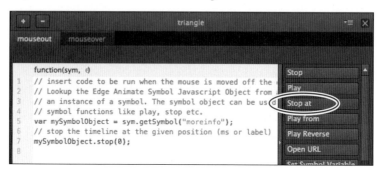

The next statement appears as follows:

```
mySymbolObject.stop(0);
```

6 Preview your Edge Animate composition in a browser by choosing File > Preview in your browser or pressing Ctrl+Enter (Windows)/ Command+Return (Mac OS).

When you roll over the triangular button at the top of the Stage, the moreinfo symbol plays its animation, which reveals the text box and text. When you roll off the button, the text box and text collapse.

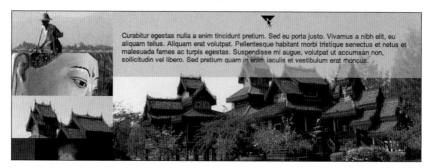

Using jQuery Effects

The Edge Animate API offers a nice balance of power, flexibility, and ease of use to incorporate inter-activity to your designs and animations. Inserting script by simply clicking a button in the script panel is (mostly) idiot-proof. However, adding a bit of jQuery to your scripts can often make your job easier. As you learned earlier in this lesson, jQuery is a JavaScript library that was written specifically to make it simple to select elements on a Web page and creating animations and transitions. There are many jQuery methods for animating elements, such as a fade-in, fade-out, or a slide-in and slide-out. Since Edge Animate is fully compatible with JavaScript and jQuery, you can use these methods wherever you see fit.

Let's examine one particular jQuery method, `fadeToggle()`. The method `fadeToggle()` animates an element's transparency to fade up or fade down, depending on its current state. If the element is transparent, it will become opaque. If the element is opaque, it will become transparent.

1   In a new Edge Animate composition, add a small rectangle and an image on the Stage. Name the rectangle **Rectangle**, and the image **Image**.

2   In the Timeline or the Elements panel, click the Open Actions button for the Rectangle element.

(continues on next page)

Using jQuery Effects *(continued)*

3   Choose click for the event.

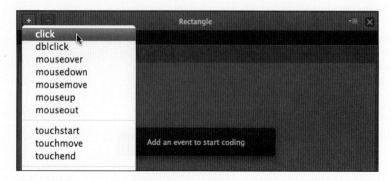

4   Add the following statement for the click event:

```
sym.$("Image").fadeToggle();
```

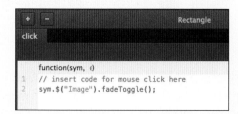

5   That's all! Preview your composition in a browser.

When you click on the rectangle, Edge Animate uses jQuery to select the image and executes the `fadeToggle()` method. The image fades in and out with alternate clicks. jQuery does all the work of creating two inverted animations without requiring you to manually create any symbols, keyframes, or mechanisms to remember the state of the image. jQuery is powerful and makes a good addition to your designer-developer toolkit. You can view the 05JQuery.an file in the 05End_JQuery folder to see the completed example.

Review questions

1   What's the difference between actions, triggers, and events, and how are they used to create interactivity in Adobe Edge Animate?

2   What's the relationship between the Edge Animate API, jQuery, and JavaScript?

3   How do you create a button?

4   Why would you use a label, and where are they located?

5   What does the code sym mean in the Edge Animate API, and how do you use it?

Review answers

1   Actions, triggers, and events are all JavaScript code that you use to create interactivity in Edge Animate. Actions are commands that tell Edge Animate to do something, such as hide or display an element, or load a hyperlink. Triggers are actions that are placed on the Timeline so they are executed at a specific time. Events are things that happen in a composition that Edge Animate can respond to with actions.

2   Edge Animate uses JavaScript to power its animation and interactivity. JavaScript is the standard scripting language for Web browsers. jQuery is a library of well-written JavaScript functions that make it easier to select and animate elements on a Web page. The Edge Animate API provides additional functions (based on JavaScript and jQuery) to control elements in your composition.

3   A button is a visual indicator of what the user can interact with. You can create a button by creating an element on the Stage, then clicking the Open Actions button in the Timeline or Elements panel to add an event. In the event tab that opens, insert actions that you want triggered when the event happens.

4   Labels are located at the top of the Timeline. Labels identify specific points in time so that you can refer to label names, rather than fixed milliseconds, in your JavaScript code.

5   The word sym represents the whole Edge Animate composition, when the statement is on the main Timeline. Edge Animate is organized around the concept of "symbols," and the root, or base-level symbol, is the Edge Animate Stage. This root symbol contains all the elements and animations in your Edge Animate composition—everything on the Stage or Timeline. In JavaScript, when you want to do something, you first identify the object that you want to control. If you want to affect the Timeline of your Edge Animate composition, the first thing that is written in the script is sym.

6 EMBEDDING MEDIA AND ADVANCED INTERACTIVITY

Lesson Overview

In this lesson, you'll learn how to do the following:

- Add events to the Stage
- Embed a YouTube video in your composition
- Embed a Google map in your composition
- Dynamically remove elements from the Stage
- Add hyperlinks
- Replace text
- Render HTML text
- Respond to keyboard presses
- Understand key codes to identify specific keys
- Handle logic with conditional statements
- Use variables
- Understand concatenation
- Program loops for repeated actions

 This lesson will take approximately two-and-a-half hours to complete. If needed, remove the previous lesson folder from your hard drive and copy the Lesson06 folder onto it.

Dive deeper in Edge Animate's JavaScript code to add
more sophisticated media and interactivity.

Getting started

To begin, view the music festival guide that you'll create as you learn to incorporate more advanced interactivity and multimedia in Adobe Edge Animate.

1 Double-click the 06End.html file in the Lesson06/06End folder to play the composition in a browser.

The project is part of a fictional interactive music festival guide. Along with the title and textual information with embedded hyperlinks, it includes an interactive Google map of the area, a music video of a featured band from YouTube, and a slideshow that you can navigate with your keyboard arrow keys.

The main buttons highlight when you roll over them, but they are non-functional.

2 Click and drag the Google map to see the surrounding area, and zoom in and out to change the scale.

3 Click on the Featured Artist button.

A YouTube video appears in the middle of the Stage while everything else dims. You can play the video to hear the music of a real band in this fictional music festival.

4 Click outside the video.

The video disappears and you return to the original music festival guide.

5 Click on the Adobe hyperlink in the introductory text.

Explore the information from Adobe that appears in the new browser window or tab. When you're done, close the window or tab and return to the music festival guide in the Edge Animate composition.

6 Click the Left or Right Arrow key on your keyboard.

New images in the slideshow appear, and the caption for each image changes to reflect the numbered image in the slideshow.

UNIVERSITY OF WINCHESTER LIBRARY

7 Close the 06End.html file and quit your browser.

8 Double-click the 06Start.an file in the Lesson06/06Start folder to open the initial project file in Edge Animate.

The Stage has already been sized properly at 1024 x 690 pixels. The file includes many of the assets already placed on the Stage. You can test the composition in a browser to see the skeleton of the project. In this lesson, you'll flesh it out by adding the interactivity and embedding the hyperlinks, Google maps, YouTube video, slideshow images, and navigation.

9 Choose File > Save As. Name the file **06_workingcopy** and save it in the 06Start folder. Saving a working copy ensures that the original start file will be available if you want to start over.

Embedding media

The Web is a wonderfully complex ecosystem, not only for its inherent ability to link sites, but for its rich multimedia elements that can be distributed widely. YouTube videos, Google maps, Flickr photo feeds, SoundCloud audio, and many other media-sharing sites offer widgets with code that you can copy and paste into your own site. With Adobe Edge Animate, you can embed many of these kinds of media into your composition, incorporating outside media and interactivity without the need to do much coding.

For your interactive festival guide, you'll embed two kinds of media to help your viewer sample the musical offerings and get themselves to the event: a Google map and a YouTube video. You'll use the jQuery method appendTo() to attach the media to existing elements on the Stage.

Creating an element for the map

The Google map shows the location of the festival, and offers integrated features such as directions, zooming, and panning for your festival attendee.

1   In Edge Animate, select the Rectangle tool and create a large rectangle on the Stage 335 pixels wide by 230 pixels high.

2   Position the rectangle at X=19, Y=440.

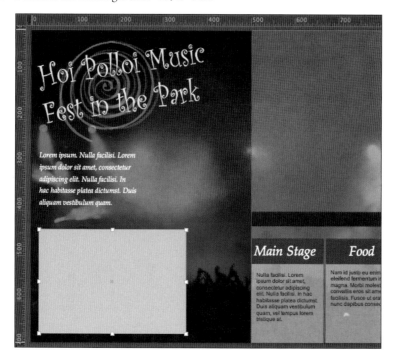

3 In the Elements or Timeline panel, rename the element **map**.

The rectangular map element serves as the container for the Google map. The color and the size won't affect the final appearance once the map is loaded, but serve only to help you position it on the Stage.

Attaching events to the Stage

Where do you actually insert the code to append the Google map to your rectangle? You insert code *not* on the element, but on the Stage itself. Your Google map should display as soon as your composition loads from the server, so you use the event called compositionReady for the Stage.

The compositionReady event happens when all the assets of an Edge Animate composition have been downloaded and the project is ready to play.

1 In the Timeline or the Elements panel, click the Open Actions button for the Stage.

The script panel for the Stage opens. A menu of options opens, displaying the events that are possible for the Stage.

2 Select the compositionReady option.

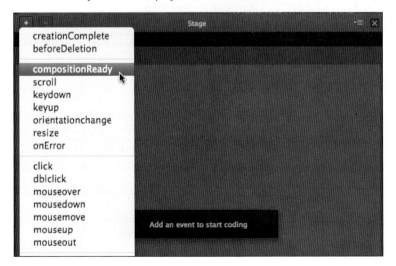

Edge Animate adds a compositionReady tab at the top of the panel with an empty script pane and available snippets on the right.

Appending a Google map

Google maps and other media-sharing sites often allow viewers to copy and paste code that uses the `<iframe>` tag. The `<iframe>` tag is an inline frame that inserts a website or a part of a website in your own site.

You'll copy the `<iframe>` code from a shared Google map and paste it in your script with an `appendTo()` statement.

1   In the compositionReady event tab of the script panel, enter the following statement:

```
sym.$().appendTo(sym.$("map"));
```

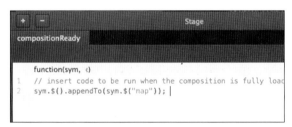

By now, you should recognize part of what the code is doing. The `sym.$()` selects certain elements, so this statement is appending something not yet defined to the map element on the Stage. Your next step is to add the iframe code within the first set of parentheses.

2 In your browser, go to Google maps at http://maps.google.com.

3 In the search field, enter **prospect park, brooklyn, ny**, and press Enter (Windows) or Return (Mac OS).

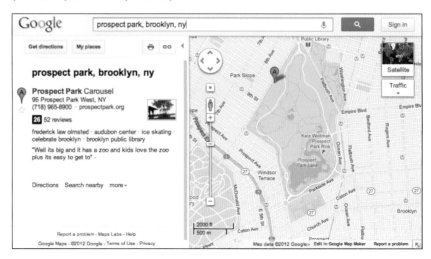

Google maps displays the area around Prospect Park, a large central park in Brooklyn, where this fictional musical festival takes place.

4 Click on the Link button.

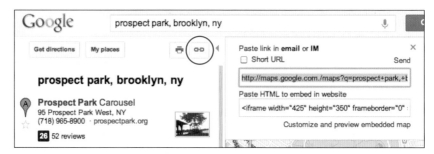

A popup window displays a direct link to the map and an iframe embed code.

5 Click on the Customize and preview the embedded map link.

A new window opens that provides additional options.

6 Select the Custom size option and enter **335** for Width and **230** for Height.

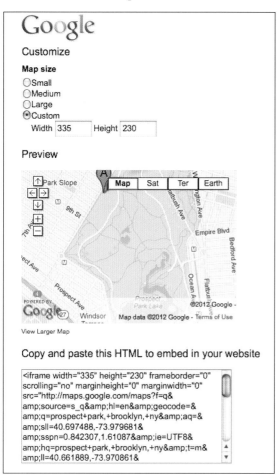

The preview map changes to the selected size, and the iframe code at the bottom of the window changes to reflect the new dimensions.

7 Place your cursor in the iframe code window and select all of its contents. Press Ctrl+C (Windows) or Command+C (Mac OS).

The iframe code is copied to your clipboard.

8 Return to Edge Animate and go back to the script panel for the compositionReady event for your Stage.

● **Note:** Any syntax errors will appear in the code error display at the bottom-right corner of the Stage and at the bottom of the Code panel. If you get errors, look carefully at your opening and closing quotes and the position of your cursor when you paste the code.

9 Place your cursor in between the first parentheses of the statement, and enter a single quote, then press Ctrl+V (Windows) or Command+V (Mac OS), and then enter a closing single quote.

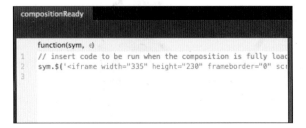

The iframe code that you copied from Google maps is pasted into the Edge Animate script panel. The script will remain on a single line, so you'll have to scroll a long way to the right to see the completed statement. Make sure that the pasted script is between single quotes.

10 Preview your composition in a browser by pressing Ctrl+Enter (Windows) or Command+Return (Mac OS).

Your browser appends the Google map search result to the rectangular map element.

● **Note:** Careful readers will notice the "View Larger Map" hyperlink below the Google map. That's part of the Google code that you copied and pasted, but you can easily remove it. Look for the ending iframe tag "</iframe>" and delete all the code from Google after that.

Showing embedded media

Now you'll add a YouTube video to your interactive festival guide. However, unlike the Google map, which is always present on the site, your YouTube video appears only when the user clicks on a button. How do you show embedded media only when you click a button?

You'll use the same jQuery method `appendTo()` that you used for the Google map to attach the YouTube video to an element on the Stage. But the `appendTo()` method will be triggered by a click event, rather than the compositionReady event, and you'll combine the statement with `show()` and `hide()` commands to create the interactivity.

This particular video interactivity requires three separate elements to work. First is the button, which responds to a click event. Second is a placeholder container, which serves as the parent element to which the YouTube video will be appended. Third is a semitransparent rectangular cover that helps create a separation between the video and the rest of the Stage by dimming all the other elements. The place-holder and the cover element are initially hidden. When you append the YouTube video to the placeholder element, you'll also reveal it and the cover element.

Creating the placeholder, cover, and button elements

You'll create the placeholder and cover elements. The button has already been created for you, and is available in the Library as a PNG image.

1   Select the Rectangle tool and create a rectangle of any color, which is 560 pixels wide and 315 pixels high.

2   Position the rectangle in the middle of the Stage at X=232 pixels, and Y=174 pixels.

3 In the Elements panel, rename the element **video**.

Your YouTube video will be appended to the video element.

4 In the Properties panel, choose Off for the Visibility.

The video element disappears from the Stage. The initial Display property for your video element is Off.

5 Select the Rectangle tool and create another rectangle that has a black fill (#000000) at 80% opacity, and is as big as the Stage at 1024 pixels wide and 690 pixels high.

6 Position the rectangle to cover the Stage at X=0 pixels, and Y=0 pixels.

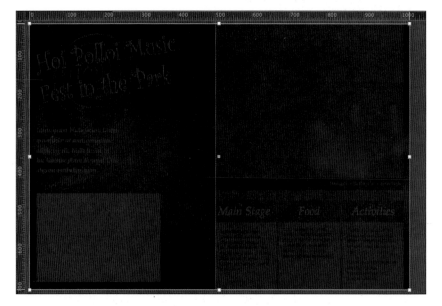

7 In the Elements panel, rename the element **cover**.

8 In the Properties panel, choose Off for Visibility.

The cover element disappears from the Stage. The initial Display property for your cover element is Off.

9 Expand the images section of your Library panel, and drag the featuredartist. png image to the Stage.

10 Position the image at X=364, Y=343.

11 In the Elements panel, rename the Symbol instance **button**.

You now have a visible button element and a hidden cover and video element.

Appending the YouTube video

1 In the Timeline or the Elements panel, click the Open Actions button for the button element.

The script panel for the button element opens, A menu of options opens, displaying the events that are possible for the Stage.

2 Select the click option.

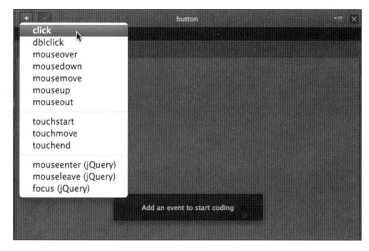

Edge Animate adds a click tab at the top of the panel with an empty script pane and available snippets on the right.

3 In the click event tab of the script panel, enter the following statement:

```
sym.$().appendTo(sym.$("video"));
```

The code is the same as the one you used to append the Google map, except you're attaching the media to the video element. Your next step is to add the YouTube iframe code within the first set of parentheses.

4 In your browser, go to YouTube at http://www.youtube.com.

5 In the search field, enter **red baraat**, and press Enter (Windows) or Return (Mac OS). You can also search for your own favorite band, if you wish.

YouTube displays search results for the real Brooklyn band that plays a fusion of Bhangra, funk, and jazz.

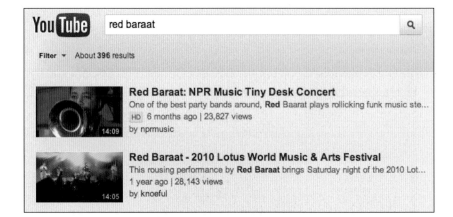

6 Choose one of the videos. The video that is embedded in this lesson is "Red Baraat in HD, Montreal International Jazz Festival."

7 Click on the Share button below the video.

A link to the video appears.

8 Click on the Embed button.

The iframe code appears for embedding the YouTube video. Additional options for resizing the video are available, but the default size works for this lesson.

9 While the iframe code is still highlighted, press Ctrl+C (Windows) or Command+C (Mac OS).

The iframe code is copied to your clipboard.

10 Return to Edge Animate and go back to the script panel for the click event for your button element.

11 Place your cursor in between the first parentheses of the statement, and enter a single quote, press Ctrl+V (Windows) or Command+V (Mac OS), and then enter another single quote.

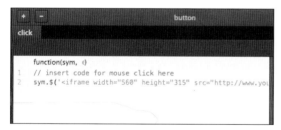

The iframe code that you copied from YouTube is pasted into the Edge Animate script panel.

12 Preview your composition in a browser by pressing Ctrl+Enter (Windows) or Command+Return (Mac OS). Click the button element on the Stage.

Nothing appears! Don't worry; your video element, to which the YouTube code is appended, is still hidden.

Showing the video and cover

Your next step is to unhide the video element.

1   In the Timeline or the Elements panel, click the Open Actions button for the button element.

The script panel for the button element opens with the click event tab.

2   On the next available line in the script panel, click Show Element from the code snippets options.

A new statement appears with the show() method that displays a selected element. The highlighted portion of the code is a placeholder that needs to be replaced.

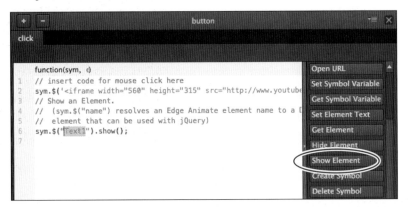

3   Replace the placeholder text, Text1, with the name of your element, **video**.

The completed statement appears as follows:

```
sym.$("video").show();
```

Edge Animate selects the element named video and executes the show() method, which reveals it on the Stage.

4   Place your cursor on the next line and choose Show Element again.

5   Replace the placeholder text with the name of your element, **cover**.

The completed statement appears as follows:

```
sym.$("cover").show();
```

Edge Animate selects the element named cover and executes the show() method, which reveals it on the Stage.

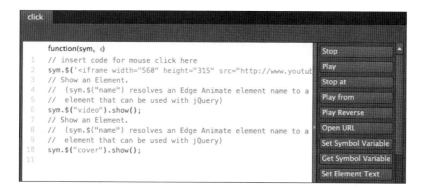

6 In the Elements panel, move the video
   element to the top of the stack, with the
   cover element just below it.

7 Preview your composition in a browser by pressing Ctrl+Enter (Windows) or
   Command+Return (Mac OS). Click the button element on the Stage.

The click event results in three actions: the YouTube video is attached to the
video element, the video element becomes visible, and the cover element
becomes visible. The result is an interactive video that floats atop your Stage.

Removing media

After your user has finished viewing the YouTube video, you want to give them the control to return to the site. Assigning a click event on the cover element provides a perfect way to trigger the actions for the return. The cover element is just below the video element and hides the entire Stage, so the cover element would capture any click off of the video.

Hiding the video requires that you use hide() for the video and cover elements as well as the method children().remove(), which removes all the elements that have been appended to another. The original element is known as the parent, and the appended elements are its children.

Removing the YouTube video

1   In the Timeline or the Elements panel, click the Open Actions button for the cover element.

The script panel for the cover element opens. A menu of options opens, displaying the events that are possible for the Stage

2   Select the click option.

Edge Animate adds a click event at the top of the panel with an empty script pane and available snippets on the right.

3   In the click event tab of the script panel, enter the following statement:

```
sym.$("video").children().remove();
```

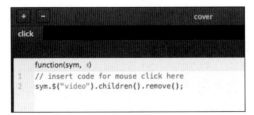

The code removes all the children elements of the video element.

Hiding the video and cover

Now you'll continue with the open script panel for the cover element.

1 In the click event tab of the script panel, choose the Hide Element from the code snippets options.

A new statement appears with the `hide()` method, which displays a selected element. The highlighted portion of the code is a placeholder that needs to be replaced.

2 Replace the placeholder text with the name of your element, **video**.

The completed statement appears as follows:

```
sym.$("video").hide();
```

3 On the next line of the script panel, choose the Hide Element option again to add another `hide()` statement for the cover element.

4 Replace the placeholder text with the name of your element, **cover**.

The completed statement appears as follows:

```
sym.$("cover").hide();
```

The final script contains three lines of code, the `children().remove()` method that removes the YouTube video, and two `hide()` methods that hide the cover and video elements.

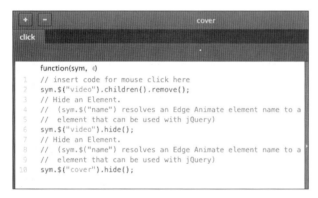

5 Preview your composition in a browser by pressing Ctrl+Enter (Windows) or Command+Enter (Mac OS). Click the button element on the Stage to append the YouTube video, then click off of the YouTube video.

The YouTube video is removed from the video element, and then the video element and the cover element are hidden from view, returning the reader to the main site.

Adding hyperlinks

The hyperlink is the backbone of the Web. It defines Web browsing because of the way it connects sites with each other. You can add a hyperlink to direct your user to link to any other site with the simple JavaScript statement window.open().

The window.open() method loads a specified URL (Uniform Resource Locator, or web address) in a new browser window or tab, or in the same browser window, if desired. The window.open() method is available in the code snippets as the Open URL option.

Adding a hyperlink for a home button

It's standard behavior for the top banner for any Web site to link back to the home page. For this interactive festival guide, you'll do the same for the title element that sits in the top-left corner of the Stage.

1 In the Timeline or the Elements panel, click the Open Actions button for the title element.

The script panel for the title element opens. A menu of options opens, displaying the events that are possible for the title.

2 Select the click option.

Edge Animate adds a click event at the top of the panel with an empty script pane and available snippets on the right.

3 On the next available line of the script panel, choose the Open URL option.

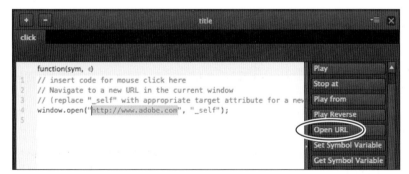

Edge Animate adds the following code:

```
window.open("http://www.adobe.com", "_self");
```

The window.open() method loads the Adobe site in "_self", which is the keyword that refers to the current browser window.

● **Note:** Use "_blank" instead of "_self" if you want to load the URL in a new browser window.

4   Replace the URL of the Adobe site with the URL of the Hoi Polloi Music Fest in the Park. Since none exists for this fictional event, you can use the code window.location.href, which refers to the URL of the current page.

The final statement should appear as follows:

```
window.open(window.location.href, "_self");
```

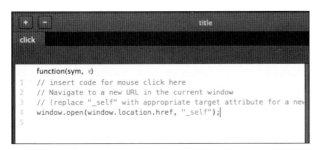

5   Preview your Edge Animate composition in a browser.

When you click on the title icon in the top-left corner of the Stage, the browser reloads the URL, which would bring the reader back to the opening state of the homepage.

Adding HTML content

The window.open() method that you learned in the previous exercise is useful for incorporating hyperlinks when clicking on elements in your composition. But if you want to insert a simple hyperlink within some text, then you need to use the html() method.

The html() method sets the contents of a text element. You can use it to replace the current contents of a text box on the Stage with new text, and you can include HTML tags within the text.

Replacing text

Your current composition includes some placeholder text that appears just under the title element. The element name for the placeholder text is called "body." After the compositionReady event fires, you'll use the html() method to replace the current text with client-approved language.

1   In the Timeline or the Elements panel, click the Open Actions button for the Stage element.

The script panel for the title element opens.

2   On the next available line in the compositionReady event, add the following statement:

```
sym.$("body").html("WELCOME. This summer, join thousands of
other revelers at Brooklyn's own Prospect Park to celebrate
the annual independent folk music festival. Made possible by
Adobe Systems, Inc.");
```

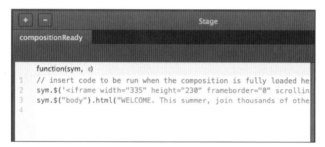

The code replaces the current placeholder contents of the body element with the text within the double quotes in the html() method.

3   Preview your Edge Animate composition in a browser.

As soon as your Edge Animate composition successfully loads, the text in the body element is replaced.

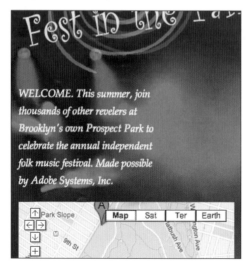

Hyperlinking text

You can add any HTML tags within the text replacement. For the body element, you'll add an anchor tag, <a>, around the words "Adobe Systems, Inc." to hyperlink them to the Adobe website.

1 Continue with the open script panel for the compositionReady event on the Stage element.

2 Revise the `html()` statement to include an anchor tag as follows:

```
sym.$("body").html("WELCOME. This summer, join thousands of
other revelers at Brooklyn's own Prospect Park to celebrate
the annual independent folk music festival. Made possible by
<a href='http://www.adobe.com'>Adobe Systems, Inc.</a>");
```

Note: Make sure that you use single quotes for the URL in the href attribute so that it is set off from the double quotes around the HTML text.

3 Preview your Edge Animate composition in a browser.

As soon as your Edge Animate composition successfully loads, the text in the body element is replaced, and the words "Adobe Systems" are hyperlinked, displaying the default blue color and underline style.

Note: Edge Animate renders any HTML with the html() method, so you can add your own formatting options, or even add additional media such as image files with the <img> tag.

WELCOME. This summer, join
thousands of other revelers at
Brooklyn's own Prospect Park to
celebrate the annual independent
folk music festival. Made possible
by Adobe Systems, Inc.

Note: If you want your URL to open in a new browser window or tab, include the attribute, `target='_blank'`, in the anchor tag. The full tag would read, `<a href='http://www.adobe.com' target='_blank'>Adobe Systems</a>`

Note: You can style the hyperlink color with inline CSS to change the default blue. For example, change the hyperlink color to red with the script `<a style='color:red' href='http://www.adobe.com'>Adobe Systems</a>`.

Keyboard events

So far in this book, you've dealt with a few different events. You explored clicks, mouseovers, and mouseouts in the previous lesson, and the compositionReady event in this lesson.

Now you'll incorporate events involving the keyboard. Edge Animate can detect whenever a user interacts with the keyboard. The keydown event happens when a key is depressed, and the keyup event happens when a key is released.

Adding the keydown event

Your music festival guide includes a short slideshow that users can navigate with the arrow keys on the keyboard. The first step in creating the interactivity for the navigation is to add a keydown event for the Stage element.

1   In the Timeline or the Elements panel, click the Open Actions button for the Stage element.

    The script panel for the Stage element opens.

2   Click on the Plus button on the upper-left corner.

    A menu of options opens, displaying the events that are possible for the Stage.

3   Select the keydown option.

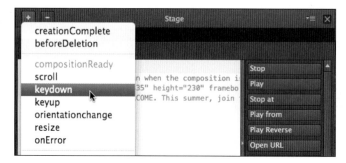

Edge Animate adds a keydown event at the top of the panel and fills it with some code, which appears as follows:

```
if (e.which == 32) {
        // do something
}
```

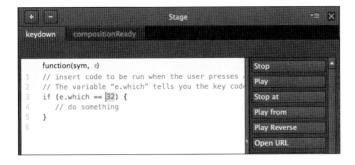

The JavaScript code that's added helps you distinguish which key was pressed. The keydown and keyup events happen when *any* key is pressed or released. In order to find out which key was pressed, we must turn our attention to conditional statements.

Handling logic with conditionals

The statement that Edge Animate added in the script pane for the keydown event is known as a *conditional* statement. It starts with the code word, if, and it includes something within its parentheses and it also contains a set of curly braces.

The conditional tests whether the statement within the parentheses is true or false. If it's true, then all the code within the curly braces is executed. If it's not true, then Edge Animate ignores any code within the curly braces.

You can think of the syntax of a conditional statement like so:

```
if (raining) {

    bring umbrella

    put on boots

    close windows

}
```

You can read this block of code logically—if it's raining, then bring an umbrella, put on your boots, and close the windows. If it's not raining, then don't do any of these tasks.

Making comparisons

Now examine the current if statement in the script panel. The condition looks like this:

```
e.which == 32
```

This statement is comparing one thing to another. This statement tests whether e.which (you'll learn about that shortly) is equal to 32. The double equal symbols mean "equivalent to." Often in conditional statements, you'll be comparing quantities. You use == to mean "equivalent," > for "greater than," or < for "less than." These symbols are known as comparison operators because they allow you to compare two different values.

Understanding key codes

What exactly is being compared in the statement e.which == 32?

The first part of the statement to the left of the double equal symbols refers to the key that was pressed during the keydown event. The variable, e, is part of an argument that is passed to the function that gets triggered when the event happens. It gets a little complicated if you're not a programmer, but the only thing you need to understand is that Edge Animate keeps track of different properties associated with each kind of event (see the sidebar "The event properties").

Every key on the keyboard has a matching code, called a *key code* or a *char code*. For example, the key code for the Spacebar is 32, and the right arrow is 39. You can easily look up the codes on the Web, and even try out interactive demos.

Since you want to create a forward and backward navigation based on the Right and Left Arrow keys, you'll add two conditional statements: one that checks if the Right Arrow key is pressed, and another that checks if the Left Arrow key is pressed.

1 Continue with the open script panel for the keydown event on the Stage element.

2 Revise the conditional statement as follows:

```
if (e.which == 39) {
    // the right key is pressed!
}
```

3 Copy the entire three lines of the conditional statement, and paste it on the next available line.

4 Revise the pasted conditional statement as follows:

```
if (e.which == 37) {
    // the left key is pressed!
}
```

Your conditional statements are almost complete. Your code, as written, checks which key is pressed, and now you can continue writing the consequences of the right or left key being pressed.

The event properties

When an event happens, Edge Animate keeps track of the different properties of the particular event in a variable called e. You can refer to this variable to tailor the response to the event. For example, for keyboard interactions, e.which of the keydown or keyup event describes the key code of the event. For mouse events, e.pageX and e.pageY describe the X- and Y-coordinates of the mouse cursor on the Stage. You can use these coordinates to make an object follow the position of the mouse cursor, for example.

Above the script panel for each event, Edge Animate displays the code function (sym, e). Click on the e, which is the variable that is passed to the function for the response to the event. A popup menu appears, which contains the various event properties that you can incorporate into your code.

UNIVERSITY OF WINCHESTER
LIBRARY

Using variables

Recognizing whether the Right or Left Arrow key is pressed is only half the story. The other half involves keeping track of how many times each key has been pressed, and displaying the appropriate image from the slideshow. To keep track of the number of times something has happened, you use *variables*. You used variables in the previous lesson so you could control symbols on the Stage. Here, you'll use variables to store a value—specifically, a number, which you can then use to display a specific image in your slideshow.

Variables are useful for any situation where you need to store information for later comparison or retrieval. Scores, the number of lives in a game, or the cost of contents of an online shopping basket are all examples of variables.

Creating variables

In Edge Animate, you create a variable using the syntax
`sym.setVariable("nameofvariable", value)`,
where the value could either be a number, a boolean (true or false), or
a string, in which case you'd enclose the characters within double quotes.

To continue creating the slideshow navigation, you'll create a variable called "counter" that is initially set to 1.

1   In the Timeline or the Elements panel, click the Open Actions button for the Stage element, if it's not already open.

2   On the next available line in the compositionReady event, choose the Set Symbol Variable option from the code snippet menu on the right side of the panel.

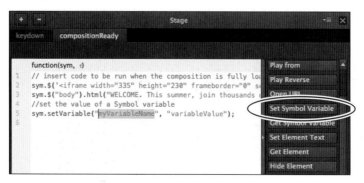

Edge Animate adds the following statement:

```
sym.setVariable("myVariableName", "variableValue");
```

3 Replace "myVariableName" with **"slidecount"** and "variableValue" with the number **1**.

Your final statement should appear as follows:

```
sym.setVariable("slidecount", 1);
```

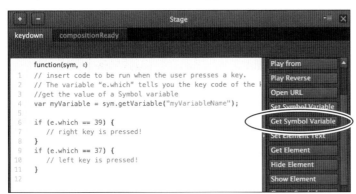

Edge Animate creates a variable named slidecount, and stores the number 1 in it.

Modifying variables

Each time your reader presses the Right Arrow key, you'll add 1 to the value of the counter variable. Each time your reader presses the Left Arrow key, you'll subtract 1 from the value of the counter variable.

You'll use that number to display the correct image from a slideshow.

1 In the Timeline or the Elements panel, click the Open Actions button for the Stage element.

The script panel for the Stage element opens.

2 Select the keydown event tab.

3 Create a new line *before* the first `if` statement, and choose the option Get Symbol Variable from the code snippet menu.

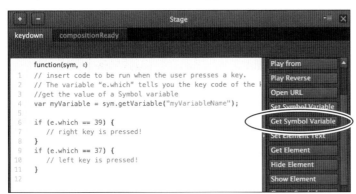

Edge Animate adds the following statement:

```
var myVariable = sym.getVariable("myVariableName");
```

4 Replace myVariable with counter, and "myVariableName" with **"slidecount"**. The final statement should appear as follows:

```
var counter = sym.getVariable("slidecount");
```

Edge Animate retrieves the value of slidecount and puts it in a variable named counter for you to access in the current script.

5 Place your cursor inside the curly braces of the first conditional statement (which tests whether the *Right* Arrow key is pressed), and enter the following line:

```
counter = counter + 1;
```

Note: You can modify the value of variables with addition (+), subtraction (–), multiplication (*), or division (/). You can also use parentheses to group the order of operations.

6 Place your cursor inside the curly braces of the second conditional statement (which tests whether the *Left* Arrow key is pressed), and enter the following line:

```
counter = counter - 1;
```

```
keydown    compositionReady

   function(sym, e)
1  // insert code to be run when the user presses a key.
2  // The variable "e.which" tells you the key code of the
3  //get the value of a Symbol variable
4  var counter = sym.getVariable("slidecount");
5
6  if (e.which == 39) {
7      // right key is pressed!
8      counter = counter + 1;
9  }
10 if (e.which == 37) {
11     // left key is pressed!
12     counter = counter - 1;
13 }
14
```

Note: A shortcut to the statement, counter=counter+1 is counter++. Similarly, instead of counter=counter–1, you can use counter– –.

Variable scope

Be aware that if you create a variable by simply stating var myvariable = 0; then that variable is only accessible in the script where it's defined. If you're thinking of creating a global variable that is accessible anywhere, you could write the statement myvariable = 0; (excluding the keyword var). However, global variables are accessible to all the JavaScript on the page, which may lead to conflicts.

It's best to stick with the statements sym.setVariable() and var myVariable = sym.getVariable() to set and get variables.

Imposing limits

Your reader could keep pressing the Right or Left Arrow keys, and the number in your variable counter could increase or decrease indefinitely. But since you have a finite number of images to show in your slideshow, you need to put some limits on the value of your variable.

You can use additional conditional statements to check if the value of counter exceeds a certain limit, and if so, you can reset its value.

1   In the Timeline or the Elements panel, click the Open Actions button for the Stage element.

   The script panel for the Stage element opens.

2   Select the keydown event tab.

3   On the next line after you increase the value of the counter variable, add the following code:

```
if(counter>5){
    counter=1;
}
```

The statement checks if the value of counter exceeds 5. If it does, it assigns the number 1 to the variable. This creates an upper limit to the variable.

```
keydown    compositionReady

    function(sym, e)
1   // insert code to be run when the user presses a
2   // The variable "e.which" tells you the key code
3   //get the value of a Symbol variable
4   var counter = sym.getVariable("slidecount");
5
6   if (e.which == 39) {
7       // right key is pressed!
8       counter = counter + 1;
9       if(counter>5){
10          counter=1;
11      }
12
13  }
14  if (e.which == 37) {
15      // left key is pressed!
16      counter = counter - 1;
17  }
18
```

4   On the next line, after you decrease the value of the counter variable, add the following code:

```
if(counter<1){
    counter=5;
}
```

The statement checks if the value of counter dips below 1. If it does, it assigns the number 5 to the variable. This creates a lower limit to the variable.

```
keydown    compositionReady

     function(sym, e)
1    // insert code to be run when the user presses a
2    // The variable "e.which" tells you the key code
3    //get the value of a Symbol variable
4    var counter = sym.getVariable("slidecount");
5
6    if (e.which == 39) {
7        // right key is pressed!
8        counter = counter + 1;
9        if(counter>5){
10           counter=1;
11       }
12
13   }
14   if (e.which == 37) {
15       // left key is pressed!
16       counter = counter - 1;
17       if(counter<1){
18           counter=5;
19       }
20
21   }
22
```

5 Finally, on the last line, *outside* both conditional statements, choose the Set Symbol Variable option from the code snippets.

Edge Animate adds the following statement:

```
sym.setVariable("myVariableName", "variableValue");
```

6 Replace "myVariableName" with **slidecount** and "variableValue" with **counter**, like so:

```
sym.setVariable("slidecount", counter);
```

```
keydown    compositionReady

     function(sym, e)
1    // insert code to be run when the user presses a
2    // The variable "e.which" tells you the key code
3    //get the value of a Symbol variable
4    var counter = sym.getVariable("slidecount");
5
6    if (e.which == 39) {
7        // right key is pressed!
8        counter = counter + 1;
9        if(counter>5){
10           counter=1;
11       }
12
13   }
14   if (e.which == 37) {
15       // left key is pressed!
16       counter = counter - 1;
17       if(counter<1){
18           counter=5;
19       }
20
21   }
22   sym.setVariable("slidecount", counter);
23
```

The last line assigns the value of counter (which has been increasing or decreasing) to slidecount so it reflects the most current value.

Coding the interactive slideshow

You've created the interplay of variables and conditionals, which keeps track of a number based on presses of the Right or Left Arrow key. Now, you'll use that number to display a particular image within a slideshow sequence.

All five images of the slideshow will be present on the Stage at the same time, but you'll show only one at a time, using the Display property. Simultaneously, you'll display a short caption that identifies the numbered image in the sequence (as "Slide 1", "Slide 2", and so on).

Concatenation

You can combine characters and numbers—an operation known to programmers as *concatenation*—to display different images and text based on your expression. For example, if the value of your counter variable is 3, you can combine it with text to be displayed, like so:

```
sym.$("caption").html("Slide "+ counter);
```

In this statement, Edge Animate selects the "caption" element, and replaces its contents with the word "Slide" and adds the value of counter. The end result is a display of "Slide 3."

You can also concatenate characters with numbers to refer to element names on the Stage. For example, consider the following statement:

```
sym.$("slideshow"+counter).show();
```

Edge Animate selects the element named "slideshow3" because it concatenates the word "slideshow" with the value of the variable counter. The method show() makes the slideshow3 element visible on the Stage.

1   Select the Text tool and drag out a text box on the Stage. For the contents of the text box, enter **"Slide 1"**.

2 Rename your newly created text element **caption**.

Your caption element will begin with "Slide 1", but will change, based on which numbered image appears.

3 Make your caption element, Georgia, Times New Roman, Times, Serif, 12 pixels, and white. Position it at X=519, Y=408.

4 Expand the images folder in the Library panel and drag the five JPG images named slideshow1, slideshow2, slideshow3, slideshow4, and slideshow5, onto the Stage.

5 Position all five images in the same position at X=501 and Y=0.

6 Change the Display property for all five images, except for slideshow1, to Off.

The first image of the slideshow is visible, while the next four are hidden.

7 In the Timeline or the Elements panel, click the Open Actions button for the Stage element.

The script panel for the Stage element opens.

8 Select the keydown event tab.

9 On the next available line in the script panel, enter the following statement:

```
sym.$("caption").html("Slide "+ counter);
```

```
     function(sym, e)
1    // insert code to be run when the user presses a
2    // The variable "e.which" tells you the key code
3    //get the value of a Symbol variable
4    var counter = sym.getVariable("slidecount");
5
6    if (e.which == 39) {
7        // right key is pressed!
8        counter = counter + 1;
9        if(counter>5){
10            counter=1;
11        }
12
13    }
14    if (e.which == 37) {
15        // left key is pressed!
16        counter = counter - 1;
17        if(counter<1){
18            counter=5;
19        }
20
21    }
22    sym.setVariable("slidecount", counter);
23    sym.$("caption").html("Slide "+ counter);
```

The statement selects the caption element on the Stage and changes its contents to identify its number in the sequence.

10 On the next line in the script panel, enter the following statement:

```
sym.$("slideshow"+counter).show();
```

```
    function(sym, e)
 1    // insert code to be run when the user presses a
 2    // The variable "e.which" tells you the key code
 3    //get the value of a Symbol variable
 4    var counter = sym.getVariable("slidecount");
 5
 6    if (e.which == 39) {
 7        // right key is pressed!
 8        counter = counter + 1;
 9        if(counter>5){
10            counter=1;
11        }
12
13    }
14    if (e.which == 37) {
15        // left key is pressed!
16        counter = counter - 1;
17        if(counter<1){
18            counter=5;
19        }
20
21    }
22    sym.setVariable("slidecount", counter);
23    sym.$("caption").html("Slide "+ counter);
24    sym.$("slideshow"+counter).show();
```

The statement selects one of the slideshow elements, based on the value of the counter variable, and changes its Display property to On so it's visible.

Loops

You're not quite done coding the interactive slideshow. If you preview your Edge Animate composition, you'll see that you can press the Right and Left Arrow keys to display the other hidden images, but all the images remain visible.

You need to add an additional piece of script that will hide all the images *except* the one you want to display.

A simple way to accomplish this is to hide them all just before turning on the Display property of the desired image. You can hide each of the images by using the Hide Element code snippet, but that requires a line of code for each image. A smarter way to do the same operation on multiple items is to use a loop.

Loops are common in programming. In JavaScript, you can use the `for()` statement, which executes a block of code over and over again, based on a set of conditions that you set. To complete the interactivity for your slideshow, you'll add a loop that hides all the images.

1   In the Timeline or the Elements panel, click the Open Actions button for the Stage element.

The script panel for the Stage element opens.

2   Select the keydown event tab.

3   Just *before* the last line of the script, enter the following statement:

```
for (i=1; i<6; i++){

        sym.$("slideshow"+i).hide();

}
```

```
function(sym, e)
 1    // insert code to be run when the user presses a
 2    // The variable "e.which" tells you the key code
 3    //get the value of a Symbol variable
 4    var counter = sym.getVariable("slidecount");
 5
 6    if (e.which == 39) {
 7        // right key is pressed!
 8        counter = counter + 1;
 9        if(counter>5){
10            counter=1;
11        }
12
13    }
14    if (e.which == 37) {
15        // left key is pressed!
16        counter = counter - 1;
17        if(counter<1){
18            counter=5;
19        }
20
21    }
22    sym.setVariable("slidecount", counter);
23    sym.$("caption").html("Slide "+ counter);
24    for (i=1; i<6; i++){
25            sym.$("slideshow"+i).hide();
26        }
27    sym.$("slideshow"+counter).show();
28
```

Let's examine each part of the code carefully. The `for()` loop has three settings in the parentheses, separated by semicolons. This statement defines a loop that starts with a variable, i=1. The loop will continue to run as long as the variable i is less than 6. The variable i will increase by 1 each time the loop runs.

The code within the curly braces runs with each loop. Note how the variable i is included in the code so that slideshow1, slideshow2, slideshow3, slideshow4, and slideshow5 become hidden after the loop finishes.

4 Preview your Edge Animate composition in a browser.

Use the Right and Left Arrow keys to navigate forward or backward through the slideshow. The correct image and caption appear based on the variable that the conditions you scripted.

Final edits

You've finished adding all the multimedia and interactivity. Your final step is to make sure that the video element and cover element remain above the slideshow images and caption. In the Elements panel, move the video element so it is at the top of the stack, and move the cover element so it is just under the video element.

Compare your project with the final composition provided, 05End.an.

Review questions

1. What is the compositionReady event, and when is it useful?

2. How do you attach a YouTube video or a Google map to your composition?

3. What are the two ways to add a hyperlink to an Edge Animate composition?

4. What are key codes, and how do you use them?

5. What's the difference between a conditional statement and a loop?

6. Why would you use concatenation?

Review answers

1. The compositionReady event is attached to the Stage, and the event happens when all the assets of an Edge Animate composition have been downloaded. Use the compositionReady event when you want to make sure that the composition is ready to play before executing a group of actions.

2. Attach a YouTube video or a Google map with the jQuery command `appendTo()`. The `appendTo()` command attaches media from iframe code to a particular element on the Stage. The element on the Stage becomes the parent, and the appended media the child.

3. You can create a hyperlink by assigning the code snippet option, Open URL, to an event on any element. For example, you can trigger the Open URL action when your reader clicks on an image on the Stage. You can also use the `html()` method to replace the contents of a text element with HTML rendered text. Use the `<a>` tag to insert a hyperlink within the replacement text.

4. Key codes are numeric values that correspond to particular keys on the keyboard. You use key codes, or char codes, to check which key has been pressed during a keydown event.

5. A conditional statement is used to check if a particular statement is true, and if it is, a group of actions are triggered. If the statement is not true, then the group of actions are ignored. Conditional statements use logic to decide whether or not a response is made. Loops also use logic, but to determine how many times a group of actions are triggered. Loops are useful for doing repetitive tasks.

6. Combining characters, numbers, or variables is known as concatenation. Concatenation allows a programmer to create dynamic references based on variables, and not fixed values or names.

7 PUBLISHING AND RESPONSIVE DESIGN

Lesson Overview

In this lesson, you'll learn how to do the following:

- Explore the various publishing options
- Publish your composition for the Web
- Add a Down-level Stage for unsupported browsers
- Capture a poster image for a Down-level Stage
- Incorporate a preloader
- Set the overflow options for your Stage
- Embed your composition into an existing HTML page
- Understand responsive design
- Make the Stage resizable
- Restrict the dimensions of the Stage resizing
- Apply percent-based layouts
- Change an element's positioning reference
- Use layout presets
- Find and use Adobe Edge Animate resources

 This lesson will take approximately one hour to complete. If needed, remove the previous lesson folder from your hard drive and copy the Lesson07 folder onto it.

Publish your Edge Animate composition to a variety of formats, or integrate it seamlessly and easily with existing Web sites. Apply responsive design techniques to make your layouts adapt to a variety of screen and device resolutions for the most optimal experience.

241

Getting started

To begin, view the fictional Urban Gardener site that incorporates an animated and interactive Edge Animate composition within a larger website.

1 Double-click the index.html file in the Lesson07/07End/Urban_Gardener_responsive folder to open the project in a browser.

   The project is a website on urban gardening. It has a straightforward layout with a title on top, a horizontal navigation bar to move between different sections, and placeholder content broken up into three columns. The Edge Animate composition is in between the top title and the main buttons. The Edge Animate composition cycles through several images, and provides buttons to navigate the images.

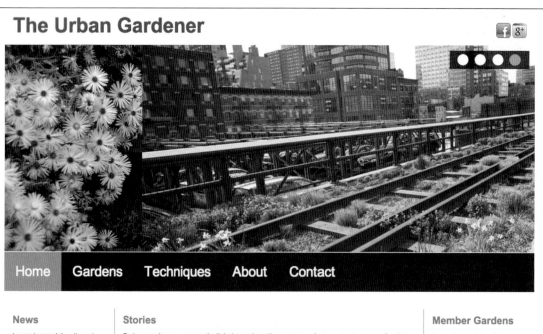

News

Lorem ipsum dolor sit amet, consetetur sadipscing elitr, sed diam nonumy eirmod tempor invidunt ut labore et dolore magna Lorem ipsum dolor sit amet, consetetur sadipscing elitr, sed

details...

Lorem ipsum dolor sit amet, consetetur sadipscing elitr, sed diam nonumy eirmod tempor invidunt ut labore et dolore magna Lorem ipsum dolor sit

Stories

Proin quam lorem, ornare vel adipiscing sed, mattis nec massa. Aenean ut ante et nunc feugiat malesuada. Vestibulum viverra, felis ut facilisis pharetra, magna odio consectetur magna, vitae adipiscing risus metus ut tortor. Morbi ut leo quam, sit amet ornare turpis. Aliquam interdum augue ac turpis porta pharetra. Nulla eget sapien quis felis feugiat luctus. Quisque euismod odio nec velit dapibus ut euismod nunc pulvinar. Phasellus ligula ante, semper eget tincidunt eu, sodales vel eros. Nunc ut quam enim. Sed semper adipiscing tincidunt.

Member Gardens

Lorem ipsum dolor sit amet, consetetur sadipscing elitr, sed diam nonumy eirmod tempor invidunt ut labore et dolore magna Lorem ipsum dolor sit amet, consetetur sadipscing elitr, sed

details...

Lorem ipsum dolor sit amet, consetetur sadipscing elitr, sed diam nonumy eirmod tempor invidunt ut labore et dolore magna Lorem ipsum dolor sit

2 Grab the bottom-right corner of your browser and shrink the width of your browser window.

The HTML elements on the page resize and become reorganized. The Edge Animate composition also adapts to the changing size of the browser window. As the window gets smaller, the images remain centered, and the buttons on the navigation bar remain a fixed distance from the right edge of the window, so they are always accessible. A layout that dynamically changes like this is known as responsive design.

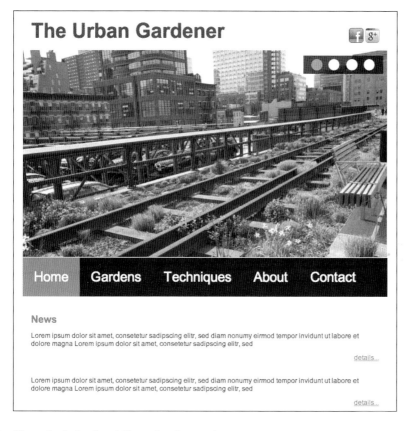

3 Close the index.html file and quit your browser.

UNIVERSITY OF WINCHESTER
LIBRARY

4 Double-click the 07Start Edge Animate file in the Lesson07/07Start folder to open the initial project file in Edge Animate. The Edge Animate composition has been completed for you. It contains all the image assets, which are animated in a loop, and all the interactivity is in place.

In this lesson, you won't be creating a new Edge Animate composition, but you will learn how to publish a nearly complete Edge Animate composition. You'll explore the different publishing options and learn to integrate an Edge Animate composition into a larger website. You'll also learn about different techniques for responsive design.

5 Choose File > Save As. Name the file **07_workingcopy** and save it in the 07Start folder. Saving a working copy ensures that the original start file will be available if you want to start over.

Publishing your composition

When you want to finalize your composition, you publish it from Edge Animate. Publishing creates all the necessary files—the JavaScript files, the HTML file, and any dependent image files—and saves them in a single folder.

Publish for the Web

By default, Edge Animate publishes files for the Web.

1   Choose File > Publish or press Alt+Ctrl+S (Windows)/Option+Command+S (Mac OS).

2   Look on your hard drive in the same folder that contains your Edge Animate source file (07_workingcopy.an).

Edge Animate creates a new folder called publish, and within that, another folder called web. Inside the web folder are all the required files. Check to make sure the following files are published:

- 07_workingcopy_edge.js
- 07_workingcopy_edgeActions.js
- 07_workingcopy_edgePreload.js
- 07_workingcopy.html
- A folder called edge_includes
- A folder called images

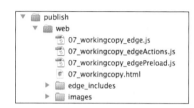

The first three JavaScript files contain code that is unique to your Edge Animate composition. The HTML file is your main document that you open in a browser. The folder called edge_includes contains the general JavaScript and jQuery functions that power the animation and interactivity. The other folder called images contains the image assets that have been copied from the main folder where your Edge Animate source file sits.

All of the files and folders within the web folder must be uploaded together for your Edge Animate composition to play over the Web.

3   Double-click the HTML file to open it, or open the file with your browser.

The Edge Animate composition plays in the browser window.

Publish options

Edge Animate provides publishing options for the Web as well as support for other formats.

1 Choose File > Publish Settings.

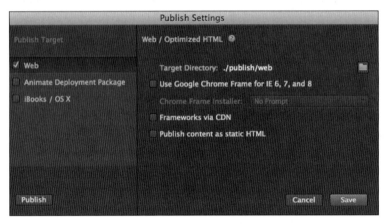

Note: You can output to multiple Publish Targets, and your Publish Settings are saved with each Edge Animate composition.

The Publish Settings dialog box appears. On the left side of the dialog box, three Publish Target options appear:

- **Web** is the default option, and publishes files for Web browsers.

- **Animate Deployment Package** publishes a .OAM file so you can import your Edge Animate composition into Adobe InDesign CS6 and use it within the Adobe Digital Publishing Suite (DPS).

- **iBooks/OSX** publishes a .WDGT file so you can import your Edge Animate composition into iBook author and publish to Apple iTunes.

2 Select the Web option.

Additional settings appear for Web export:

- The Target Directory is the location of your published files. Click the Folder icon to change the target directory.

- **Use Google Chrome Frame for IE 6, 7, and 8** publishes your Edge Animate compositions so they can be viewed on non-HTML5 browsers such as Internet Explorer 6, 7, and 8 with Google Chrome Frame, an open-source downloadable plug-in for IE.

- **Frameworks via CDN** publishes your files with a reference to a hosted JavaScript library. Edge Animate uses the JavaScript library on Google (http://ajax.googleapis.com/ajax/libs/jquery/1.7.1/jquery.min.js) for the CDN, which stands for Content Distribution Network.

- **Publish content as static HTML** publishes your composition so your elements are exposed in the HTML markup, and not hidden in JavaScript. If you compare the HTML document of your Edge Animate composition published with and without this option enabled, you'll see how the text is visible on the HTML page, which makes the content more accessible to search engines. Your composition remains animated, however, as "static" refers to how the content is rendered, and not whether animation is supported.

Controlling the Stage Display with Overflow options

When you publish your Edge Animate composition and view it in your browser, you may discover that the elements that extend off your Stage are still visible. Edge Animate controls the display of items off the Stage with the Overflow property. The Overflow options are available in the Properties panel when the Stage is selected.

The options are as follows:

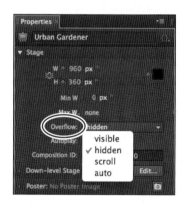

- visible, which shows all elements on or off the Stage.

- hidden, which only shows content within the Stage.

- scroll, which adds browser scroll bars to the Stage.

- auto, which adds browser scroll bars to the Stage when content spills off the Stage.

For the most part, you'll want to choose hidden for your Overflow option, which will ensure that your animations play as you intend. In our Urban Gardener animation, for example, the images slide onto the Stage from off-Stage on the right. The hidden Overflow option hides the images until it moves over the Stage. Change the Overflow options and preview the composition in a browser to see how the content displays.

Down-level Stage

A Down-level Stage is the appearance of your composition when it is displayed in a non-HTML5, older browser. Edge Animate provides a way to show a static image instead of your animated, interactive composition.

It's good practice to create a Down-level Stage to offer alternate content to your viewers who are using older browsers.

Creating the Down-level Stage

You access the Down-level Stage through the Properties panel for the Stage element. For this interactive slideshow, you'll choose a static image.

1 Click the Stage element in the Elements panel to select it.

2 In the Properties panel, click the Edit button for the Down-level Stage.

Edge Animate takes you to the Down-level Stage, indicated by navigation bar at the top of the Stage.

Most of the Timeline and Tools are grayed out. For a Down-level Stage, you are limited to static images and text. Edge Animate provides an alert in the middle of the Stage that you haven't yet set up a Down-level Stage.

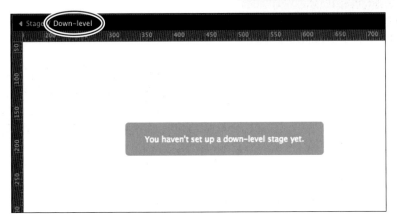

3 Drag the photo1 file from the images folder in the Library onto the Stage. Position the image at X=0, Y=0.

The photo1 image appears on the Stage. This image will be displayed as the alternate content if your reader's browser doesn't support the animation and interactivity.

4 Choose the Text tool from the Tools panel.

5 Click on the Stage to insert text. Enter a short message for the readers of non-supported browsers.

Notice that your two elements (the photo and the text) appear in your Elements panel as child elements of a Down-level symbol.

You can manage the stacking order of your Down-level Stage by dragging items within the Elements panel, just as you can in the main Stage.

6 Click on the Stage link above the Down-level Stage.

You return to the main Stage. You can visit the Down-level Stage at any time to make further edits.

Saving a poster image

If you've created an animation, you can capture a single frame from the animation to be displayed on your Down-level Stage. The static image from your animation is known as a Poster image.

1   Move the playhead to 0:02.250 seconds, at the point when the photo2 is sliding over the Stage and partially covering photo1.

2   Click the Stage element in the Elements panel to select it.

3   In the Properties panel, click the camera icon next to Poster.

A dialog box appears with a choice to capture a poster image at the current location of the playhead, or to refresh the poster image with a new image at a different playhead location.

4 Click the Capture button.

Edge Animate creates a Poster image of the Stage at 0:02.250 seconds and saves the image as Poster.png in your Library panel.

Note: Remember that the Poster.png file actually resides in the images folder on your hard drive. To delete a Poster image, right-click the Poster.png item in the Library panel and choose Reveal in Finder. Delete the file from your hard drive and its reference in the Library panel will be removed.

5 Click the Edit Down-level Stage button in the dialog box that remains open.

Edge Animate takes you to the Down-level Stage, where you can use the Poster image from the Library panel in your Down-level Stage composition. Click the Insert button in the Properties panel to automatically place the Poster Image on the Down-level Stage.

Note: Your Edge Animate composition must be saved on your hard drive in order to create a Poster image.

For this lesson, keep the current Down-level Stage as is. In this slideshow, a still image is a more appropriate Down-level Stage than a Poster image that shows two images in mid-transition.

Revising a poster image

You'll probably make edits to your composition, which means you'll have to update your Poster image. Edge Animate provides options for easily revising your Poster image.

1   Move the playhead to a new location on the Timeline at 0:07.250 seconds.

2   Click the Stage element in the Elements panel to select it.

Note: Click the Seek marker in the Capture a Poster Image dialog box to automatically move the playhead to the time of the last Poster image capture.

3   In the Properties panel, click the camera icon next to Poster.

A dialog box appears with a choice to capture a poster image at the current location of the playhead, or to refresh the poster image with a new image at a different playhead location.

Capture a Poster Image

Capture a static .png image of the stage that can be used for down-level browsers and when publishing.

Capture a new poster image at the current playhead position. A new file will be created and remembered as the poster image.

[Capture]

Overwrite the current poster image with a fresh capture.

[Refresh]   Seek to 0:02.250

4   Click the Refresh button.

Edge Animate captures a new Poster image at 0:07.250, overwriting the one that you created at 0:02.250 seconds.

Adding a hyperlink

Elements on your Down-level Stage can be hyperlinked so readers from unsupported browsers can be directed to additional content. For example, you could link them to non-HTML5 content, or you could lead them to download a supported browser.

1   Edit your Down-level Stage, if you're not already there.

2   Select the text element on your Stage.

3   In the Properties panel, choose newWindow for the Link Target, and enter **http://www.google.com/chrome** for the Link URL.

Your text on the Down-level Stage is hyperlinked to Google Chrome's download website, which will open in a new tab or window.

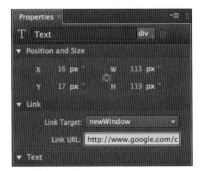

Properties

T Text   div

▼ Position and Size

   X   16 px   W   113 px
   Y   17 px   H   119 px

▼ Link

   Link Target: newWindow
   Link URL: http://www.google.com/c

▼ Text

4   Return to the main Stage.

Preloaders

The file size of your composition can quickly become bulky when you include many assets, especially items like elaborate SVG artwork or large images. Even with a high-speed Internet connection, a big file can take time to download.

While there's no definition of what's too big, it's always a good idea, regardless of the size of your composition, to provide a preloader for your readers. A preloader is simply a visual indicator of the download process. Some preloaders can provide actual information about the amount of data received, such as the horizontal bar or the dial that fills up when you download files from the Web. Others are simpler, and just provide an indication of ongoing activity, such as a spinning wheel.

Adding a preloader

Edge Animate provides several simple preloader graphics for you to use.

1   Select the Stage element in the Elements panel.

2   In the Properties panel, click the Edit button for Preloader.

Edge Animate takes you to the Preloader Stage, indicated by the navigation bar at the top of the Stage.

Most of the Timeline and Tools are grayed out. The alert in the middle of the Stage tells you that you haven't yet set up a preloader.

3 Click the Insert Preloader Clip-Art button and choose a preloader graphic from the pull-down menu. Click Insert or double-click your selection.

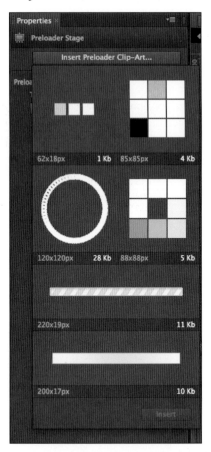

The Preloader graphic appears centered on the Stage. The Preloader graphic, an animated GIF, is saved to your images folder and appears in the Library.

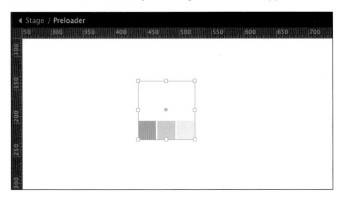

4 Return to the main Stage and preview your composition in a browser.

Your preloader appears momentarily, just before the slideshow for your Urban Gardener site begins. All the assets for your composition load quickly since you are previewing it locally (directly from your hard drive). When all the assets for your project are uploaded to your Web server, your readers will appreciate the preloader graphic, which will remain until all assets have completely downloaded.

The Preloader code and the graphic itself add to the size of your overall composition. Edge Animate displays the file size of each graphic (ranging from 1 Kb to 10 Kb), and the total size of your Preloader (code plus graphic) in the Properties panel of your Preloader Stage.

Note: In the Properties panel of the main Stage, your Preloader can either be set to Immediate or Polite. The Immediate option makes your composition load the code libraries and image assets as soon as possible. The Polite option makes your composition wait until the Web page's onload event happens.

Note: You can use your own Preloader graphic if you import your own animated GIF or other artwork by choosing File > Import, or pressing Ctrl+I (Windows)/Command+I (Mac OS).

Embedding your composition into HTML

So far you've added a Down-level Stage, a Preloader, and checked the Overflow option for your Stage, and now you're ready to integrate your final Edge Animate composition into a larger HTML site.

Edge Animate keeps your composition's code modular, so it's a relatively easy matter to insert your interactive slideshow to an existing website.

Inserting the runtime code and Stage

In the 07Start lesson folder, you've been provided a sample website called "The Urban Gardener." The simple home page represents a fictional informational site on gardening for the city dweller. You'll replace the static top banner image with the interactive slideshow made with Edge Animate.

1 Open the Urban_Gardener folder to examine the documents inside.

The index.html file is the main document that opens in your browser. The css folder contains a CSS document to style the website, and the images_urbangardener folder contains the image assets.

2 Double-click the index.html file to open the Web site in a browser.

The Urban Gardener site contains a static header image of the New York skyline with a view of some rooftop gardens.

3 In Edge Animate, publish your 07_workingcopy composition again, with the preloader and Down-level Stage added.

Your final published files appear in the folder called web inside a folder called publish.

4 In a text editor or an HTML editor such as Adobe Dreamweaver, open both the index.html file for the Urban Gardener site and the 07_workingcopy.html file for your Edge Animate composition.

5 In the 07_workingcopy.html document, copy all the code between the `<!--Adobe Edge Runtime-->` opening tag and the `<!--Adobe Edge Runtime End-->` closing tag that appears just before the closing `</head>` tag.

```
 1    <!DOCTYPE html>
 2    <html>
 3    <head>
 4        <meta http-equiv="Content-Type" content="text/html; charset=utf-8">
 5        <title>Urban Gardener</title>
 6    <!--Adobe Edge Runtime-->
 7        <script type="text/javascript" charset="utf-8" src="07_workingcopy_edgePreload.js"></script>
 8        <style>
 9            .edgeLoad-EDGE-94802810 { visibility:hidden; }
10        </style>
11    <!--Adobe Edge Runtime End-->
12
13    </head>
14    <body style="margin:0;padding:0;">
15        <div id="Stage" class="EDGE-94802810">
16        </div>
17    </body>
18    </html>
```

The script represents the Adobe Edge Animate runtime. It points to the JavaScript file that contains the code that powers the animation and interactivity. The code that you should copy appears as follows:

```
<!--Adobe Edge Runtime-->

<script type="text/javascript" charset="utf-8"
src="07_workingcopy_edgePreload.js"></script>

<style>

.edgeLoad-EDGE-94802810 { visibility:hidden; }

</style>

<!--Adobe Edge Runtime End-->
```

6   In the index.html file, paste the code that you just copied in the head of the document (in between the opening <head> and the closing </head> tags).

```
1    <!DOCTYPE HTML>
2    <html>
3    <head>
4    <meta charset="utf-8">
5    <meta name="viewport" content="width=device-width, initial-scale=1.0">
6    <title>The Urban Gardener</title>
7    <!-- css3-mediaqueries.js for IE8 or older -->
8    <!--[if lt IE 9]>
9        <script src="http://css3-mediaqueries-js.googlecode.com/svn/trunk/css3-mediaqueries.js"></script>
10   <![endif]-->
11   <link href="css/styles.css" rel="stylesheet" type="text/css">
12 ▼ <!--Adobe Edge Runtime-->
13       <script type="text/javascript" charset="utf-8" src="07_workingcopy_edgePreload.js"></script>
14       <style>
15           .edgeLoad-EDGE-94802810 { visibility:hidden; }
16       </style>
17 ▲ <!--Adobe Edge Runtime End-->
18
19   </head>
20
21   <body>
22
```

7   Return to the 07_workingcopy.html file and copy the <div> element that represents the Edge Animate Stage. The <div> element has the id attribute of "Stage" and the class attribute matches the composition ID from the Edge Animate Properties panel.

```
1    <!DOCTYPE html>
2    <html>
3    <head>
4        <meta http-equiv="Content-Type" content="text/html; charset=utf-8">
5        <title>Urban Gardener</title>
6    <!--Adobe Edge Runtime-->
7        <script type="text/javascript" charset="utf-8" src="07_workingcopy_edgePreload.js"></script>
8        <style>
9            .edgeLoad-EDGE-94802810 { visibility:hidden; }
10       </style>
11   <!--Adobe Edge Runtime End-->
12
13   </head>
14   <body style="margin:0;padding:0;">
15 ▼     <div id="Stage" class="EDGE-94802810">
16 ▲     </div>
17   </body>
18   </html>
```

The code that you should copy looks similar to this:

```
<div id="Stage" class="EDGE-94802810">
</div>
```

8 In the index.html file, paste the code to replace the <div> tag containing the headerPic.jpg image.

The code that you should replace is as follows:

```
<div class="headerPic"><img src="images_urbangardener/
headerPic.jpg" alt="" width="960" height="360"></div>
```

```
4    <meta charset="utf-8">
5    <meta name="viewport" content="width=device-width, initial-scale=
6    <title>The Urban Gardener</title>
7    <!-- css3-mediaqueries.js for IE8 or older -->
8    <!--[if lt IE 9]>
9        <script src="http://css3-mediaqueries-js.googlecode.com/svn/t
10   <![endif]-->
11   <link href="css/styles.css" rel="stylesheet" type="text/css">
12   <!--Adobe Edge Runtime-->
13       <script type="text/javascript" charset="utf-8" src="07_workin
14       <style>
15           .edgeLoad-EDGE-94802810 { visibility:hidden; }
16       </style>
17   <!--Adobe Edge Runtime End-->
18
19   </head>
20
21   <body>
22
23       <header class="container">
24       <div class="headerTop">
25           <h1>The Urban Gardener</h1>
26           <ul class="socialIcons">
27               <li><a href=""><img src="images_urbangardener/faceboo
28               <li><a href=""><img src="images_urbangardener/googleI
29           </ul>
30       </div>
31 ▼     <div id="Stage" class="EDGE-94802810"></div>
32       <nav>
33           <ul id="navlist">
34               <li id="active"><a href="#">Home</a></li>
35               <li><a href="#">Gardens</a></li>
36               <li><a href="#">Techniques</a></li>
37               <li><a href="#">About</a></li>
38               <li><a href="#">Contact</a></li>
39           </ul>
40       </nav>
41       </header>
```

Copying the code libraries and assets

Your Edge Animate composition depends on the various JavaScript libraries and image assets, so your next step is to copy them over to the Urban_Gardener folder.

1 Copy the three JavaScript documents 07_workingcopy_edge.js, 07_workingcopy_edgeActions.js, and 07_workingcopy_edgePreload.js from the publish/web folder to the Urban_Gardener folder.

2 Copy the edge_includes folder and all of its contents from the publish/web folder to the Urban_Gardener folder.

3 Copy the images folder and all of its contents from the publish/web folder to the Urban_Gardener folder.

4 Open the index.html file from the Urban_Gardener folder in a browser.

The Urban Gardener site opens. Your interactive, animated slideshow replaces the static image as the top banner.

Making revisions to your composition

When you edit your composition, be aware of which files in the integrated site need to be updated.

- If you change the layout, animation, or interactivity, replace the three JavaScript files in the folder that contains your index.html document.

- If you add, delete, or modify the image assets in your composition, replace the images folder with your updated images folder.

Note: As long as your Edge Animate Composition ID remains the same, you won't have to modify any of the scripts you copied and pasted into the index.html document.

About responsive design

Responsive design is an approach to website layouts that make it possible to respond to different sizes of the browser window. Normally, when browser windows are resized, their contents don't change that much. When the browser window is made wider, the content may be kept centered, but nothing more. When the browser window is made narrower, scroll bars often appear.

Responsive design takes into account the dimensions of the container in a much smarter way. Elements within the window may not only re-center, but they can be resized, remain fixed at certain positions, or be entirely rejiggered to account for the altered real estate.

Adobe Edge Animate makes it easy to create responsive designs by giving you options for percentage or pixel-based positioning and sizing to take into account the different platforms and devices with a variety of screen resolutions. Edge Animate also provides a way to test out the effects of resizing the Stage directly within the Edge Animate application.

Looking at responsive design

The Urban Gardener site is set up to adapt to changes in the browser window, but your Edge Animate composition in the top banner does not.

1 Open the index.html document in a browser.

2 Drag the bottom-right corner of your browser window to make it bigger and smaller.

As the window becomes wider, the site remains centered.

As the window becomes smaller, the elements within the window change. When the window becomes smaller than 960 pixels, the three columns start squeezing in proportionally so they all remain visible, with no horizontal scrolling required.

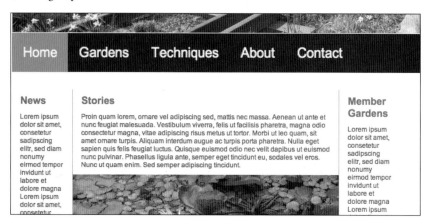

As the window reaches an even smaller width, the three columns disappear and the columns become stacked, one on top of the other. As the window gets smaller still, the buttons in the top horizontal navigation bar are resized.

Your Edge Animate composition, on the other hand, remains a fixed width, so the images are cut off by the shrinking browser window. The buttons to navigate the images completely disappear.

Making the Stage scalable

The first step in making your composition responsive to size changes is to change the Stage settings for its Width and Height.

1   Open the 07_workingcopy Edge Animate file and select the Stage in the Elements panel.

2 In the Properties panel, click the unit toggle for Width.

The units for the Stage width change from 960 pixels to 100%. The contents of the Stage will now fit the width of its container (the browser window).

3 Preview your composition in a browser (Command+Enter/Ctrl+Enter), and resize the browser window.

The contents of the Stage now fill the browser window horizontally. Even the images that are off the Stage to the right are now visible.

4 Close your browser window and return to Edge Animate.

Previewing size changes

Edge Animate lets you preview how size changes in the browser window affect the contents of your Stage without having to leave the application.

1 When the Stage Width or Height units are set at percentages, stage resize handles appear on the ruler.

Note: To display the rulers, choose View > Rulers or press Ctrl+R (Windows)/ Command+R (Mac OS).

2 Drag the stage resize handle on the horizontal ruler back and forth.

The Stage resizes and shows what would appear on the Stage at any particular width. The exact pixel values for the Width show up near the stage resize handle. Note how the off-Stage images appear as they did when you previewed it in the browser.

Restricting maximum and minimum dimensions

Since the images off to the right of the Stage appear when the container is resized wider than 960 pixels, you'll want to restrict its maximum width. Use the Max W and Min W properties to constrain the width.

1 In the Properties panel, click on Max W and deselect the None option.

The value of the current width of the Stage appears. The Stage resizing is now restricted to a maximum of 960 pixels.

2 Enter **960** for the value of Max W, and keep the units at pixels

The Stage resizing is now restricted to a maximum of 960 pixels.

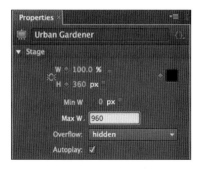

3 Drag the Stage resize handle on the top ruler.

You can make the Stage smaller, but the Stage can't be resized past 960 pixels. The off-Stage elements remain dimmed, indicating that they aren't visible.

Percent-based layouts

The point of responsive layouts is to change the contents on your Stage to best accommodate its size. You can make the size of objects on the Stage be a percentage of the container rather than a fixed pixel value to dynamically respond to size changes.

You'll modify the image-size settings so they don't get cut off when the container is made narrower.

1 In the Elements panel, hold down your shift key and select all the photo elements (photo1, photo2, photo3, photo4, and photo1Copy).

2 In the Properties panel, click the unit toggle for W in the Position and Size section.

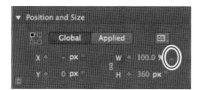

3 In the Background Image section, click the unit toggle next to H.

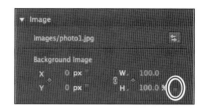

The units for the width and height for the selected images change from 960 pixels to 100%.

When you drag the Stage resize handle, the width of all the images varies with the container width. However, the height is fixed. The result is a distortion of the images.

4 While all of the images are still selected, click the H property in the Background image section of the Properties panel, and enable the Auto option.

The Auto option for Background image forces the Height dimension to remain proportional to its Width dimension (or vice versa).

Now when you resize the width of the Stage, the full width of the images remain visible (because their widths are set at 100%), *and* they are kept in proportion because their Height properties for Background image are set to Auto.

One problem remains. The images shrink relative to the top-left corner, leaving a wide black margin at the bottom. One approach is to force the Y position of the images to also be a percentage, rather than a pixel, value.

5 Click the unit toggle for the Y property in the Background image section of the Properties panel.

6 Enter 50% for the value of Y.

The vertical positions of the selected images are forced to be at 50% of the height of the window.

When you resize the width of the Stage, the images shrink in proportion and are kept at the middle of the Stage. The black background appears at the top and bottom, much like the letterbox effect of widescreen movies on television sets.

7 Preview your composition in a browser and resize the browser window to see the effects of the percentage-based layout.

Relative positioning

Now turn your attention to the buttons in the upper-right corner of your composition. The buttons get cut off as the browser window becomes narrow, but you need to keep them visible to adapt to the changing size of the window.

You can maintain the position of objects relative to any corner of the Stage by using the coordinate space picker in the Properties panel. By choosing the upper-right corner of the coordinate space picker for the group of buttons, you can keep them at a fixed distance, or a proportional distance, from the right edge of the window.

1 In the Elements panel, select the Group element, which contains the four buttons that navigate the slideshow.

2 In the Position and Size section of the Properties panel, click the upper-right corner of the coordinate space picker.

The Group element is now measured relative to the top-right corner of the Stage.

3 Drag the resize Stage handle to make the container narrower.

When you resize the width of the Stage, the group of buttons remains at a fixed distance from the right edge.

Global and applied coordinates

Next to the coordinate space picker in the Properties panel are two options, Global and Applied. You can choose to view and set the position and size of your elements in either mode. In Global mode, the coordinates are calculated relative to the Stage. In Applied mode, the coordinates are calculated relative to the selected element's coordinate space. For example, select the Group element in your Elements panel.

In Global mode, its position is displayed as X=806 pixels, Y=10 pixels. Those values refer to its position from the top-left corner of the Stage.

Now click on the Applied mode. The position coordinates change to R=10 pixels, T=10 pixels, which reflects its own coordinate space, where it is 10 pixels from the right edge and 10 pixels from the top edge of the Stage.

Layout presets

With so many options for positioning and resizing, it can be challenging to configure the correct properties for your desired responsive design. To simplify the process, Edge Animate provides a menu of presets for common resizing behavior for images.

1 In the Elements panel, hold down the Shift key and select all the photos.

2 In Position and Size section of the Properties panel, click the Layout Preset button.

The Layout Preset dialog box appears with six preset options.

3 Select the Center Background Image and click Apply.

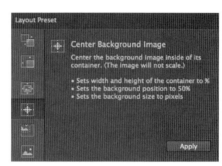

Your selected elements are fixed at 960 pixels by 360 pixels, and their X and Y coordinates are kept at 50% of the container. The combination of options prevents the letterbox effect, and instead, makes the images remain centered (but cropped) as the container is resized.

Explore some of the other preset options to see how resizing changes the layout.

4 Publish your final composition and update the three JavaScript files in the Urban_Gardener folder to integrate the latest changes to your composition.

Both the Edge Animate composition in the header and the surrounding HTML elements in the final Urban Gardener website adapt to the changing dimensions of the Web browser. When you make the window narrow, the Web site's columns rearrange themselves, the slideshow images are re-centered, and the buttons remain in the upper-right corner, so your reader always has access to the image navigation.

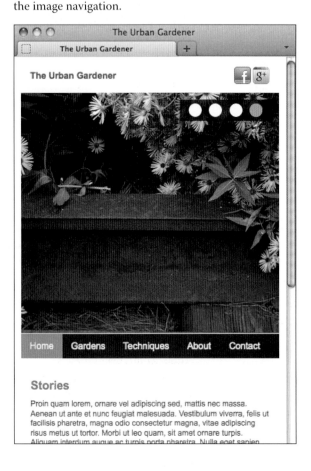

Layout defaults

When creating and positioning new elements, the default settings are to use pixels as units and to have the upper-left corner as the point of reference. You can change the default settings in the Layout Defaults panel, accessible from the Tools panel just above the Stage.

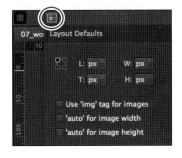

Other layout options include using <img> tags for images, and setting the width and height properties to auto.

The layout defaults are saved with each Edge Animate file, and are not preferences for the application. (So, new files always default to pixel units and upper-left corner referencing).

Edge Animate resources

Congratulations! You've made it through all seven projects, and in the process, learned how to import images and create eye-catching graphics, add complex animation, integrate interactivity and rich media, and finally incorporate responsive design and publish your masterpiece.

You've completed these projects, many of them from scratch, so you know how the various tools, panels, and JavaScript code work together.

But there's always more to learn. Continue the learning process by exploring Adobe Edge Animate's main site (http://html.adobe.com/edge/animate/). Watch experts guide you through tutorials on Adobe TV (http://tv.adobe.com/). Learn more about the Edge Animate API to delve deeper into complex interactivity (http://www.adobe.com/devnet-docs/edgeanimate/api/current/index.html). Lastly, join the thriving and growing community of fellow Edge Animate users— learning is fun and more efficient when you have others to share your successes and frustrations (http://forums.adobe.com/community/edge_animate).

You can access many of these resources directly via links from the Help menu within the Edge Animate application.

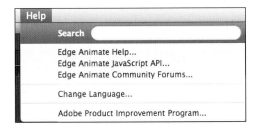

Review questions

1 What files does Edge Animate create when you publish your composition for the Web?

2 What is a Down-level Stage and how are poster images used for a Down-level Stage?

3 How do you insert your composition into an existing website?

4 What is responsive design?

5 What's the difference between Global and Applied coordinates?

Review answers

1 When you publish your composition for the Web, Edge Animate creates a folder called publish with a subfolder called web. Contained within the web folder are all the necessary files that you need to upload to your server. The final published files include three JavaScript files, the main HTML file, a folder called edge_includes, and another folder called images (if your composition contains imported images).

2 A Down-level Stage is the appearance of your composition when it is displayed in a non-HTML5, older browser. You can include images and/or text in your Down-level Stage. You can also create a Poster image, which is a screenshot of your Stage at any time along the Timeline to capture a particular point in your animation. It's good practice to create a Down-level Stage to offer alternate content to viewers using older browsers.

3 To insert your composition in an existing website, you have to copy and paste the Adobe Edge Animate runtime from the Edge Animate HTML document into the destination HTML document. The runtime appears within the <head> of the HTML document, and points to the JavaScript file that contains the code that powers all the animation and interactivity. You also have to copy and paste the <div> tag that contains your Edge Animate Stage. The <div> contains the unique ID that refers to your composition. Finally, the JavaScript files, the edge_include folder, and any dependent image assets must be moved to the destination HTML directory.

4 Responsive design is an approach to website layouts that makes it possible to make content respond to the changing size of the browser window. Adobe Edge Animate provides tools for responsive design by allowing percentage-based positioning and sizing, and options to change the positioning reference for each element.

5 In Global mode, Edge Animate calculates the coordinates for an element relative to the top-left corner of the Stage. In Applied mode, Edge Animate calculates the coordinates relative to the selected element's coordinate space, which may be different, depending on which corner point is being used as the reference for positioning.

INDEX

SYMBOLS

" (double quotation mark), 166, 180
' (single quotation mark), 166, 223
* (asterisk)
    next to filename, 12
    using as multiplication operator, 230
( ) (parentheses), 166
+ (addition operator), 230
– (subtraction) operator, 230
. (dot) operator, 166
/ (division operator), 230
/* */ (multiline comments), 167
; (semicolon), 167
< (less than operator), 226
== (equivalent operator), 226
> (greater than operator), 226
@font-face rule, 63
\\ (backslash characters), 134, 164, 167
{ } (curly braces), 225

A

<a> (anchor) tag, 223, 239
actions
    about, 199
    adding to events, 171–172
    defined, 162
    executing after events, 162, 167
    triggers as, 162
    using conditional statements to trigger or
        ignore, 239
Add Keyframe icon, 34
Add Web Font dialog box, 64–66, 91
addition (+) operator, 230
Adobe
    information and resources from, 5–6, 271
    training and certification programs by, 6
    Web tools offered by, 2
Adobe Community Help, 5, 271
Adobe Edge Animate
    creating compositions in, 12
    further resources on, 5–6, 271
    Global and Applied modes for, 272
    graphics compatible with, 17
    installing, 3
    jQuery's uses in, 161–162, 197–198, 199
    overview of, 1–2
    previewing Stage size changes in, 263
    rendering HTML in, 223
    responsive design in, 272
    starting, 10–11
    undoing steps in, 38
    using JavaScript in, 160–161, 199
    workspace for, 13
Adobe Edge Animate Classroom in a Book
    copying lesson files for, 3–4
    prerequisite skills for, 2–3
Adobe InDesign CS6, 246
aligning
    elements with Smart Guides, 18
    grouped elements with Distribute, 71–72
alpha channel, 46
Alt/Option key, 61
.an files, 11
anchor <a> tag, 223, 239
animated banner ad. *See* banner ad
animation. *See also* assets; designing animation;
        nested animation; symbols
    about, 83
    adding to symbols, 128–132
    adjusting timing of, 37–38, 94
    animating leaf rotation, 78
    changing element height and width, 99
    copying, 109
    copying, pasting, and editing symbol instances,
        137–139
    defined, 28
    easing motion in, 112–114, 119
    fade-in and fade-out effects, 102–105
    lengthening or shortening, 36–37, 92–93,
        117–118, 132–135
    looping, 132–135
    nested, 124–128
    pasting, 110–111
    reversing, 105
    shadow, 149–150
    swapping assets in, 107
    uses for clipping in, 147, 155
.ansym files, 144, 151
appending
    Google maps, 207–210, 239
    YouTube video, 211–217, 239
appendTo( ) method
    appending YouTube video with, 211, 239
    linking Google maps with, 207
Applied coordinates, 268, 272
Applied mode, 272
arguments
    defined, 164
    method, 166

scale (continued)
changing element, 97–99
indicator for smooth animation for
change, 101
making Stage scalable, 261–262
script panel
copying <iframe> code to, 209–210
hiding video and cover elements
from, 219
linking iframe embedded code to,
207–210
selecting button elements from,
213–214
slideshow counter concatenation in,
233, 236
viewing options for, 165
scripts
adding comments in, 134, 164
adding jQuery effects in, 197–198
making global edits to, 189
sym in, 166, 199
viewing code for, 165
scrubbing, 31
selecting
all property lanes of elements, 109
center of rotation, 76–77
element group, 71
multiple and noncontiguous files, 44
text fonts, 23
semicolon (;), 167
Send to Back option, 25
Shadow property, 149–150
shadows. See drop shadows
Share button (YouTube), 214
Shift key
constraining elements with, 50
selecting multiple files using, 44
shortening animations, 36–37, 92–93
single quotation mark ('), 166, 223
skewing rectangles, 53–54
slideshow. See also interactive
compositions
concatenating slides and captions for,
233–236
navigating with arrow keys, 224–225,
226–233
Smart Guides
disabling, 18
positioning image on Stage with, 85
using, 59
snapping
elements to guides, 58
playhead to keyframes, 30
spacebar, 88
stacking order of Down-level Stage, 249
Stage
animating symbols on, 128–132
attaching events to, 206–207, 239
copying, pasting, and duplicating
elements on, 61
deleting image file from, 45
dragging images from Library panel
to, 145

entering Symbol editing mode
for, 126
exiting Symbol editing mode,
127–128
having element appear abruptly on,
96–97, 119
illustrated, 9, 13
images moving from bottom
of, 145
making scalable, 261–262
offering Down-level, 248–249, 272
Overflow option controlling display
on, 247
percent-based layouts for, 264–267
placing multiple instances on, 135
poster images for, 250–252, 272
relative positioning of objects on,
267–268
removing YouTube video from, 218
responding to mouse cursor, 160
revising poster images, 252
setting properties for, 14, 15–16
zooming in/out of, 14
starting. See also enabling
Edge Animate, 10–11
stopping. See also disabling
nested animations, 139–140
playhead at designated time,
171–172
stopwatch icon, 29, 39
String names in JavaScript, 180
styling
hyperlink color, 223
text, 60–61
subtraction (−) operator, 230
SVG files
about, 43
browsers supporting SVG fonts, 68
importing, 48
JPEG vs., 79
scaling images, 50
swapping, assets, 107
sym, 166, 199
symbol animation
adding, 191–193
playing, 193–195
resetting, 195–196
symbol instances. See instances
symbols
about, 17, 45, 124
animating, 128–132
changing rotation direction of, 136
controlling animation in
JavaScript, 191
converting elements to,
124–126, 155
creating looping animations
inside, 155
deleting and duplicating, 144
editing in Library panel, 141–143
editing mode for, 126, 127–128
editing on Stage, 126–128
enabling nested animation with, 124

importing, 144, 151
instances vs., 155
placing animations inside, 126–127
Playback options for, 126, 139, 155
playing animation for, 193–194
sharing between Edge Animate
files, 144
Stage as root symbol, 199
working with instances of, 135–136
synchrony of symbol instances, 135
syntax
coding JavaScript trigger, 166–167
conditional statement, 225
reviewing errors in appended Google
map, 210
system requirements for Edge Animate, 3

T

tags
<a>, 223, 239
<iframe>, 207–210
<img>, 271
<link>, 66
television series website
adding angle to roll of tape,
129–130
adding characters to Stage, 145–149
animating roll of tape across Stage,
128–144
creating nested animation for,
124–128
lesson files for, 122–123
revising animation for, 154
rotating roll of tape, 126–127
title banner for, 147–148
text
adding hyperlink tags within
replaced, 223
adding moving title, 88–90
animating, 28–31
applying web fonts to, 67
color of, 61
creating, 22–24
duplicating, 61
editing, 62
element tags for, 18
hyperlinking, 223
label, 60
moving in opposite direction from
image, 88–90
replacing content using html( )
method, 221
replacing placeholder, 216
setting width of text box, 62–63
styling, 60–61
thumbnails
adding colorized button, 181–182
hiding colorized, 183
inserting mouseover event to
grayscale, 183–186
mouseout events for colorized,
186–188

time. *See also* timing
  lengthening or shortening animation,
    36–37, 92–93, 117–118,
    132–135
  removing, 93
time markers, 30
Timeline
  adding labels to, 178–179
  adding trigger to symbol's,
    133–135, 155
  animating elements from Pin to
    playhead, 86–88
  changing label references in
    JavaScript, 180–181
  collapsing and hiding elements on,
    106–107
  easing motion in, 112–114, 119
  inserting keyframes on, 34–35
  keyframes on, 83
  locking and hiding elements on,
    26–27, 39
  opening actions for YouTube button
    element, 213–214
  playback controls for, 32
  snapping behavior for, 30
  stopping playhead at designated time
    on, 171–172
  symbols using separate, 124
  using triggers on, 162
  zooming in/out of, 106
Timeline panel
  about, 26
  illustrated, 9, 13
timing
  adjusting with keyframes, 37–38
  editing selected portions of
    animation, 117–118
  modifying total length, 115–116
titles
  adding moving, 88–90
  easing in and out, 112–114
Tools panel, 13
training and certification programs, 6
Transform tool, 51–52, 79
transformations
  applying to all or single elements of
    group, 71
  changing origin of scale, 99–101, 119
  effects available on elements, 79
  flipping instance to change rotation
    direction, 136
  setting origin of rotations in, 76–77
transitions
  inverting changes made with Pin
    tool, 105
  pasting, 111
  smooth, 83

transparencies, 46
triggers
  actions and events vs., 199
  adding code to composition with,
    162–164
  adding to symbol timeline,
    133–135, 155
  click events triggering appendTo()
    method, 211
  coding syntax for, 166–167
  defined, 132–133, 162
  displayed in Code panel, 174
  editing, removing, and deleting, 165
  triggering looping animations, 155
TTF (True Type Font) format, 68
turning on/off. *See* enabling; disabling

U

Undo command, 38
ungrouping elements, 73
unsaved changes, 12
Urban Gardener project. *See* publishing
  compositions
URLs (Uniform Resource Locator)
  adding link to home page, 220
  opening in new browser
    window, 223
  using single quotes in href
    attribute, 223

V

variable scope, 230
variables
  creating, 228–229
  creating dynamic references based
    on, 239
  e, 227
  imposing limits in conditional
    statements, 231–233
  limiting number of loops
    with, 237
  modifying, 229–230
  using, 228
vector graphics, 47–48
video
  appending YouTube, 213–216, 239
  removing YouTube, 218
  unhiding video and cover, 216–217
  viewing on Stage, 14
visibility
  Display property and element,
    94–97, 119
  displaying elements vs. managing
    Stage, 27

W

warning messages, 144
web fonts
  adding to animation, 91–92
  adding to Library panel,
    64–67
  applying, 67, 79
  refining text after applying, 68
  types supported by browsers, 68
  using Google, 63, 64–65
web subfolder, 272
websites. *See also* responsive design;
    television series website
  adding links to other, 220–221
  adding runtime code and Stage for
    embedded, 255–258
  embedding on your own site, 207
  inserting compositions into
    existing, 272
  publishing compositions
    for, 245
width
  adjusting Stage, 15
  animating changes in element, 99
  linking height and, 49
window.open() method, 220–221
wipes, 147, 155
word spacing, 51
workspace. *See also* Stage; Timeline; *and
    specific panels*
  illustrated, 13
  saving custom panel
    arrangements, 13
  Stage, 14

X

X/Y values, 19

Y

YouTube video, 211–219
  appending, 213–216, 239
  removing, 218
  unhiding video and cover,
    216–217

Z

zooming in/out
  adjusting rotation center point
    with, 77
  of Stage, 14
  of Timeline, 106

UNIVERSITY OF WINCHESTER
LIBRARY

WATCH
READ
CREATE

Unlimited online access to all Peachpit, Adobe Press, Apple Training and New Riders videos and books, as well as content from other leading publishers including: O'Reilly Media, Focal Press, Sams, Que, Total Training, John Wiley & Sons, Course Technology PTR, Class on Demand, VTC and more.

No time commitment or contract required! Sign up for one month or a year. All for $19.99 a month

SIGN UP TODAY
peachpit.com/creativeedge